MW01717169

THE PRODIGY WITHIN

The Quest to Discover Your Life's Purpose

for late bloomers and other seekers

WAYNE ROBERT LEHRER

THE PRODIGY WITHIN

The Quest to Discover Your Life's Purpose

for late bloomers and other seekers

WAYNE ROBERT LEHRER

Published by:

PRODIGY WITHIN PUBLISHING

1112 Montana Ave. #506
Santa Monica, CA. 90403
www.prodigywithin.com

SAN 857-0780

For more information and resources for discovering your life's purpose, speaking services, coaching, workshops, seminars and other products visit our website at **www.prodigywithin.com**

Copyright © 2008 by Wayne Robert Lehrer

Printed in the United States of America

All rights reserved. No part of this book may be reproduced or transmitted in any form or by any means, electronic or mechanical, including photocopying, recording or by any information storage and retrieval system without written permission from the publisher, except for the inclusion of brief quotations in a review.

Library of Congress Control Number: 2008935443
Library of Congress Cataloging-in-Publication
The Prodigy Within: The Quest to Discover Your Life's Purpose
1. Self-Help 2. Motivational 3. Spirituality I. Title
ISBN 978-0-9820135-0-2

Cover Concept: Wayne Robert Lehrer
Cover Art & Graphic Design: Rebekah Albrecht
Cover Illustration: Bruce Bermudez

"… and I said to the almond tree,

'Sister speak to me of God,'

and the almond tree blossomed."

Nikos Kazantzakis

CONTENTS

PART I

The Quest To Discover Your Life's Purpose

PART II

Liberating The Prodigy Within – The 7 Principles of Prodigy

CHAPTER 1

THE QUESTION, THE QUICKENING AND THE QUEST

THE QUESTION

One of the single greatest causes of unhappiness, stress and disease is that most people have not discovered the gift that is theirs alone to give: their calling, their life's purpose.

Questions such as, "Who am I?" "What am I here for?" and "How can I be of service?" are no longer the sole province of spiritual seekers. Instead, these are the questions asked by each of us who has not found true satisfaction in the acquisition of power, fame, and fortune, has watched "forever" institutions, like marriage, crumble, or has wondered why we should spend the rest of our lives doing work we don't love and pursuing goals that no longer have meaning for us.

Consider that baby-boomers and future generations will have from seven to ten professions over the course of their lives. Life expectancy is rising toward 100 years. People are coming out of retirement repeatedly and others are returning to school again and again. It becomes obvious why the need to discover our calling—our life's purpose—has become the collective Quest of our generation.

> *There is in man a fate that lends power to his life. And if he succeeds in assigning the right place to life and the right place to fate, thus bringing the two into harmony, he puts his fate on a firm ground.*
>
> *"I CHING"*
> *Translated by*
> Richard Wilhelm

Until the 20th Century, the average person received little or no education, began work by age 10, had children by 15 (and all the responsibilities that accompany them), rarely experienced life beyond their home town, and could expect to die by their 46th birthday.

In the 21st Century many of us have the extraordinary privilege of spending the first quarter of our lives in school, choosing our livelihood, starting our families in our 30s or 40s, changing professions a half-dozen times, and retiring at age 65 (or younger) with a number of healthy and active years still before us. Until recently there were no such things as continuing education, changing fields, personal growth or the "Golden Years."

With these extraordinary opportunities available, it is no longer justifiable to consider yourself a failure if you haven't figured out what you want to be by the time you're 20, and haven't achieved it by your 40s or even 50s. Many innate gifts require the synthesis of a lifetime of work and experience to reveal the full extent of one's innate possibilities. Just as a caterpillar gives no hint of the beautiful butterfly it is to become, most of us have only a vague idea of our true potential and the unexplored aspects of ourselves waiting to blossom. The pre-50-year-old Gandhi gave little indication of the gift he was yet to give.

As someone engaged in his eighth profession, give or take one or two, I know this Quest all too well. I've been an accomplished filmmaker, entrepreneur, health professional, inventor, yoga teacher, business consultant, and multi-media designer for television, World's Fairs and museums. Yet, in spite of my extensive accomplishments, I've always felt that I had yet to put it all together. In conversations with friends and business associates I discovered that I was not alone. I've heard the exact same story, the same yearning, from people of all ages and every walk of life. I've heard it not only from those who have stumbled from job to job, but also from those who have achieved the kind of success, professionally and financially, that the rest of us dream about. In fact, it has become increasingly obvious to me that our generation is heeding a silent, unprecedented, evolutionary call to become all that we can be, and to discover a way to share that gift with our fellow human beings.

> *Your soul yearns for the highest experience of itself it can imagine. It came here for that purpose, to realize itself; that is, make itself real in its experience.*
>
> *"Conversations With God: Book 3"*
>
> Neale Donald Walsch

THE QUICKENING

A Quickening is taking place in the world. Trips across the continent that used to take months now take hours; calculations that required weeks are made in seconds; communications that traveled via horseback a hundred years ago now travel at the speed of light; new ideas that might have taken months, years or centuries to disseminate can be distributed to every corner of the earth instantaneously. On top of this, the population of the planet will double in less than 30 years; species are becoming extinct at the rate of over 10,000 per year; entire forests are disappearing daily; and toxic wastes are finding their way into our land, air and water at a rate that is incalculable. While all of this is happening, we humans are trying to simply get on with our personal lives as though everything were right on track. But it is becoming increasingly difficult to deny the effects of this acceleration and the numerous ways in which it is bleeding into our personal world.

> *It's never to late to be what you might have been.*
>
> George Eliot

So where does that leave us? It leaves us at the ultimate crossroads between the ongoing evolution of our species and our planet. We are poised on a precipice where, if we do not evolve collectively, we may not evolve at all. In order for the evolution of the "Human Experiment" to continue on this planet we must make a collective leap from the I-Me-Mine consciousness of Darwin to the planetary consciousness of We-Us-Ours. Though many people continue to deny that we are rushing toward self-induced destruction, the rapidly gathering weight of scientific facts and projections has become increasingly unavoidable. The stakes are high—nothing short of potential annihilation. We are so "evolved" that we have the ability to eradicate ourselves almost instantaneously; nuclear explosion, fallout, lasers from space, airborne viruses, man-made toxins and strains of bacteria that are impervious to every drug are some of the disasters that face us. Beyond that, there are still the growing threats of starvation, pesticides, war, nerve gas, weather, worldwide droughts, climate change and more.

With all this in mind there is an entirely different aspect of the Quickening to be considered: the Quickening that is occurring in the spiritual aspect of our lives, that spiritual traditions have prophesized would arrive in the "Final Days." As we race toward the void, individuals are experiencing this Quickening as a Call to confront the self-centered lifestyle that has brought us to this point. They are answering the Call to assume responsibility for our planet, the human race, and the other species that call earth home. Those who choose to respond to the Quickening by embodying their Calling will find the necessary energy and inspiration they require to accelerate their personal evolution, integrate their psyches, and receive the guidance they need to become the right person, in the right place, at the right time. It is foretold that when a significant number of individuals make the Decision to be of service to the greater good, we can reverse the direction of our collective momentum from the self-destructive path we have been unconsciously generating and make the quantum leap to the next phase of evolution: peace on earth.

> *In every artist's development the germ of the later work is always found in the earlier. The nucleus around which the artist's intellect builds his work and himself… changes little from birth to death.*
>
> Edward Hopper

THE QUEST

In the myth of Parsifal and the Quest for the Holy Grail is revealed the archetypal journey each of us must ultimately undertake to liberate the prodigy within, reveal the gift that is ours alone to give, and discover our life's purpose.

As the legend goes, the King (the Higher Self) and the Land (Humanity and the Earth) are one. King Arthur is dying from a festering wound, and Britain has become a stagnant wasteland. The country is in a state of absolute chaos; hunger, violence, starvation, disease and despair have a stranglehold on the land and the people. The only hope for the salvation of the King and the country lies in discovering the Holy Grail, the Cup of Destiny (our life's purpose). The Grail Cup, purported to contain the waters of everlasting life, is capable of healing all wounds with a single drink. The King knows the only hope for his country, his people and himself lies in discovering the mysterious Grail Castle (the Castle Perilous), obtaining the Chalice and drinking of the Holy Grail. He sends the Knights of the Round Table on the ultimate Quest. The myth states that the Castle Perilous exists in the spirit world and can only be located by one who is guided by the benevolent intent that accompanies an open heart and pure spirit. Within the Castle the wounded Fisher King has guarded the Cup of Destiny for over 800 years, awaiting the arrival of a truly worthy Knight who must ask The Question, "Whom does the Grail serve?" (Also interpreted "What ails thee humanity?" or "How may I be of Service?") Charged with King Arthur's challenge, the 12 Knights of

> *This is the true joy in life, the being used for a purpose recognized by yourself as a mighty one ... the being a force of nature instead of a feverish selfish little clod of ailments and grievances complaining that the world will not devote itself to making you happy.*
>
> George Bernard Shaw

the Round Table—including Parsifal, the Perfect Fool—ride off in search of the Holy Grail.

As Legend has it, each of the Knights strikes off in a different direction. Several perish along the way, some are lost or broken, and still others return empty handed and filled with shame. Parsifal alone, his innocence and purity his sole guide, is magically led to the mysterious Grail Castle. Once inside he comes face to face with the ailing Fisher King and within arms length of the Grail Cup (his destiny). Overwhelmed by the celestial display that accompanies the arrival of the Grail, Parsifal reaches out for the Cup. Overcome by his great good fortune and dazzled by the opportunity to save his world, Parsifal forgets to ask the question. Inches from victory, the Cup, the Castle, and the Fisher King disappear before his very eyes. To his great astonishment and anguish, Parsifal finds himself in the real world. A world he, in his innocence and self-centered desire, was unable to perceive before. Shattered by the recognition of his greed and resulting failure Parsifal's eyes are opened to a world of pain, disease and hopelessness. For the next seven years (some accounts say twenty) Parsifal's Shattering deepens as he wanders through the Wasteland that had once been Britain, haunted by the knowledge that he could have saved his King and his country rather than plunging it deeper into destruction and despair. When Parsifal finally returns to Camelot, the sight of King

> *An unemployed existence is a negation worse than death itself, because to live our lives means to have something definite to do … a mission to fulfill … and in the measure in which we avoid setting our life to something, we make it empty … Human life, by its very nature, has to be dedicated to something.*
>
> Jose Ortega y Gasset

Arthur on his deathbed strikes the final blow.

As he describes the fate of the other Knights, all hope fades from Arthur's face. Being the great King that Arthur is, he praises Parsifal for doing all that any man possibly could. Parsifal, however, knows that when it really counted, he failed his King. With this painful revelation, his Shattering is complete.

In the moment that he stands before his King (Higher Self) and takes responsibility for his failure, Parsifal makes The Decision: The Decision to dedicate his every waking moment to finding his way back to the Grail Castle (the Spiritual world). He promises Arthur he will never sleep in the same bed for more than one night and will not return home until he has obtained the Cup of Destiny.

> *It is more important to find out what you are giving to society than to ask what's the right means of lievelihood.*
>
> J. Krishnamurti

As fate would have it, unforeseen forces soon guide Parsifal once again to the Grail Castle. This time, however, as the Grail mysteriously appears, Parsifal gathers his wits and asks The Question that every one of us must ask: "Whom does the Grail serve?" ("How may I be of service?"). In a blinding flash the Castle is illuminated by an otherworldly light, angels' voices fill the air, and the vault of the heavens open. Parsifal stands transfixed as the holy visage of the Grail descends, the Waters of Everlasting Life overflowing into an ailing world. Parsifal rises into the air and is anointed by the Holy Grail. Then, just as suddenly as it all began, the light fades, the angelic voices subside, and the Castle evaporates into the mist. Parsifal awakens to a transformed world: the Land is restored, the inhabitants are renewed and the King is healed.

A new age is born.

- The Stages of the Quest

Parsifal's Quest to discover the Holy Grail represents a precise map that depicts the personal quest, sacrifice, and transformation each of us must undertake to liberate the prodigy within and reveal our life's purpose. This journey can be understood in The Stages of the Quest.

STAGE ONE: The Call to the Quest

> *Right livelihood is work that genuinely develops us as we develop it.*
>
> Lama Surya Das

The Call to the Quest usually occurs on our first trip into the world in our 20s and 30s. In the first stage, we respond to The Call by dedicating ourselves to excelling, achieving, and acquiring. Though we are motivated, to an extent, by a higher cause, we are primarily motivated by the ego's need to prove itself. We believe we act alone and anointed—motivated by the intention to win, at any cost. As we respond to The Call, our personal goals lead us to individuate and develop self-sufficiency by acquiring knowledge, honing our skills, and exploiting our talents. Though we are often committed to benign and benevolent objectives, we are primarily self-directed, striving for victories and yearning for rewards (money, power and prestige). In Parsifal's life, The Call is represented by his departure on the quest, motivated by the desire to prove himself, be knighted, and gain the gifts that accompany victory.

STAGE TWO: The Shattering

The Shattering happens in mid-life (anywhere from late 30s to the 50s) when we realize, after attaining many of our personal goals and becoming aware of our numerous failures, that much of what we have achieved seems painfully empty, meaningless, and self-centered. As we open to these feelings, the old self begins to shatter in what is often referred to as a mid-life crisis. In Parsifal's quest, The Shattering occurred when he realized that, even though he alone made it to the Grail Castle, his blind, self-centered desires caused his failure and put his king and country in grave peril.

Intent is a force that exists in the universe. When sorcerers … beckon intent, it comes to them and sets up the path of attainment, which means that sorcerers always accomplish what they set out to do.

"The Active Side of Infinity"
Carlos Castaneda

STAGE THREE: The Decision

The Decision occurs when we realize that, although we have had some degree of success in our life, we have failed (miserably in many cases) at creating anything of real value or making any contribution to the world around us. As this feeling of failure and heartbreak fills us with remorse, we are moved to make The Decision to discover our life's purpose and live for "the highest good for all." Parsifal reached The Decision as he came face to face with the dying King Arthur, the suffering of humanity, and the devastation that strangled Britain. In that moment of Decision, Parsifal committed never to rest until he had fulfilled his calling.

STAGE FOUR: The Question

In The Question stage, we ask, "Whom does the Grail serve?" Our Quest shifts from striving to fulfill our own egoistic needs to feeling the pain of humanity, experiencing the world's needs, and responding to the Call that touches our heart. When we shift to asking The Question, we begin to let go of the past, show up to the full intensity of the present, and commit our future to discovering, developing, and fulfilling our life's purpose. As our commitment is tested and our desire to serve deepened, we are miraculously guided to our destiny. As Parsifal was purified of his selfish and egotistical motivation, benevolent forces guided him to the Cup of Destiny once again. This time however he was not overwhelmed by the ego's desire but truly moved by his desire to discover, "What ails thee humanity? How may I be of service?"

STAGE FIVE: The Answer

The Answer is given as we strive to discover the highest and best in ourselves and offer it graciously to fulfill the need in the world that we feel we can best effect. The Answer is most often revealed in ever-expanding opportunities to be "who I was always meant to be."

We know, for the first time, that we are fulfilling our life's purpose, serving an important function in our world and blessed beyond measure by our giving. For Parsifal, The Answer was given when he selflessly returned to the Quest motivated only by a desire to serve the needs of his king, his fellow humans, and the earth itself. With The Answer came redemption, renewal, and Knighthood—a spiritual rebirth.

While the era of Knighthood has passed, the spirit of the Quest is as true today as it was then. The following pages of this book con-

CHAPTER 2

INVITATION TO THE QUEST

WHAT IS THE PRODIGY WITHIN®?

The Prodigy Within refers to the driving force that propels each of us to develop his or her unique purpose in life—to become the person we are meant to be. The Prodigy Within is a guide for the Quest to discover our calling. For many of us, the prodigy is hidden deep within us like sealed orders, waiting for the moment when we are finally ready to embrace it. At that time, our distinct constellation of talents, ambitions, and abilities becomes the raw material of the exceptional gift that is ours alone to give.

Though prodigies have come to be defined primarily as children born with an extra-ordinary talent, the premises of this book are:

1. Within each of us is a power, a force and a presence: I call it the prodigy. The prodigy exists within us as a drive, like the id, the

ego and the superego. The prodigy is the presence that compels us to evolve, to be all that we can be.

2. Behind every job we've held, every class we've taken, and every interest we've explored, the prodigy has been quietly guiding our steps, nurturing our talents, assembling our skills, and developing the conditions to become the center of our lives, our work, and our world. The prodigy guides us to discover, develop, and embody our calling.

> *If you follow your bliss, you put yourself in a kind of a track that has been there all the while, waiting for you, and the life that you ought to be living is the one you are living. When you see that, you begin to meet people who are in the field of your bliss, and they open the door to you. I say follow your bliss, and doors will open where you didn't know they were going to be.*
>
> *"The Power of Myth"*
>
> Joseph Campbell

3. As we develop our gift and its avenues for expression we experience an ever-expanding joy, a new sense of freedom, and a powerful momentum toward self-actualization. In this process we discover that the aspects of our self (personality) we previously considered "negative" are nothing more than frustrated expressions of a thwarted desire to realize our true selves. By integrating the "7 Principles of Prodigy" into our life, these "negative" qualities are, over time, transformed and integrated. As this occurs, our gifts, our personality, and our desire to be of service are unified into our life's calling.

Author's Note: Psychologists see the process of therapy as one of growth toward a more integrated psyche, purposeful life, and loving existence. Though a huge portion of therapy strives to tap into the drive to uncover one's purpose in life, psychologists have never identified and named that force within us in the same way that Freud identified the id, ego and superego. This idea of a positive, spiritual element within man has most often been relegated to religious foundations. Modern psychology has alluded to the process of integration; Abraham Maslow's Hierarchy of Needs, Erik Erikson's 8 Stages of Psychosocial Development and Carl Jung's collective unconscious each acknowledge and value the internal regenerative process, but still they have not identified the internal force—the prodigy—that motivates the evolution and integration of the Self. James Hillman, author of *The Soul's Code*, comes closest to naming this presence that guides us to our calling with his description of the *daimon*, something he equates to a guardian angel. Though there is ultimately no way to know whether we are compelled to evolve because of an internal motivating force, the prodigy, or an external source of motivation, the *daimon*, it is essential that we take responsibility for discovering and embodying our calling by attuning our hearts and minds to its ever-present wisdom and guidance.

> *And the day came when the risk to remain tight in a bud was more painful than the risk it took to blossom.*
>
> Anais Nin

• The 7 Principles of Prodigy: Manifesting Your Calling

Genius commonly refers to someone born with extraordinary intelligence (IQ), whereas prodigies are measured by what they do, create, or produce. A genius can become a prodigy, but prodigies don't have to be geniuses. When you consider people like Mozart, Einstein, Mother Teresa, and Tiger Woods, it is obvious that each of these prodigies were far more than their genetic code. They were the product of their environment, passion, commitment, and mentors.

As stories of everyday late-bloomers will confirm, rare child prodigies aside, most prodigies manifest their gift as a result of extensive training, support, and determination. After years of research, I've distilled the character traits of prodigy into The 7 Principles of Prodigy. These 7 Principles offer a simple, straightforward, and easily applicable roadmap for seekers dedicated to manifesting their prodigy; they also act as a guide for parents wishing to develop the prodigy within their children.

> *In the middle of the road of my life I awoke in a dark wood, where the true way was wholly lost . . . .*
>
> Dante Alighieri

The 7 Principles of Prodigy are an action plan for generating the focus, drive, and circumstances necessary to realize the full potential of the prodigy. The 7 Principles are presented in the order of their natural unfolding, leaving it to the reader to decide which Principles are most important to focus on. Once you recognize the high price you have paid by focusing on your strengths to avoid developing your weaknesses, the 7 Principles of Prodigy present a valuable antidote, by which you can 1) acknowledge any imbalance in your ability to employ the 7 Principles and 2) focus on developing these weak links by applying the Principles and use the appropriate Prodigy Practices (found in *The Prodigy Workbook*).

As the dynamic equilibrium between the 7 Principles is re-established, the intuition (ability to hear the voice of the prodigy within) is heightened. Your intentions start to manifest effortlessly and your calling begins to organically reveal itself.

• The 12 Archetypes of Service – The Way You Share Your Calling With the World

Over the years that I've assisted people in manifesting their prodigies, it has become apparent that many who were absolutely sure of their gift remained trapped in a struggle to earn their living sharing it with the world. At first I didn't understand this phenomenon, believing, as Marsha Sinetar's book states, Do What You Love and the Money Will Follow. However, over time I discovered that it is not enough to know what your gift is or to be doing it. In order to experience real satisfaction in life, you must ultimately develop the means to share it with the world in a way that is appropriate for your personality. The 12 Archetypes of Service offers exactly this, an elegant and enlightening way to assess and discover how each of us needs to give our gift. When we connect our gift with our appropriate Archetypes of Service, we begin living our calling.

For example, if your gift is physics, you can share it through the Archetype of The Explorer, like Einstein; The Problem Solver, like Enrico Fermi; or The Mentor, as do thousands of gifted high school teachers. Of course most of us are a combination of two or more of these Archetypes. The likelihood of achieving success is increased significantly when we activate the Archetypes that resonate with our personality and spirit. I am now convinced that until individuals successfully unite their gift with their Archetypes, they will never fully experience their calling and what Abraham Maslow refers to as self-actualization.

• The 12 Archetypes of Service:

THE ALTRUIST I Give, I Serve, I Love

THE WORKER I Do, I Work, I Maintain

THE EXPLORER I Seek, I Discover, I Excel

THE ACTIVIST I Believe, I Voice, I Change

THE ARTIST I Reveal, I Design, I Create

THE COLLABORATOR I Enhance, I Contribute, I Engage

THE NURTURER I Share, I Care, I Nourish

THE LEADER I Lead, I Guide, I Direct

THE MENTOR I Teach, I Support, I Inspire

THE PERFORMER I Express, I Entertain, I Uplift

THE HEALER I Heal, I Enhance, I Renew

THE PROBLEM SOLVER I Organize, I Resolve, I Explain

• A Contemporary Path to Self-Actualization

The existing definition of prodigy as a singular talent of unequalled measure, exhibited primarily by children, is giving way to a new and far more compelling definition: prodigy as the agent for the transformation (and unification) of the self.

You may be familiar with the portrayal of Mozart in the film *Amadeus* as a tempestuous, spoiled child. Others like Van Gogh, Orson Welles, Frieda Kahlo and Picasso are often depicted as arrogant, sickly, or insane. Though it is true that many prodigies have been forced to live on the fringe of society, defend themselves ferociously and adapt to reality to realize their dreams; there are legions who have not only flourished, but represent the best of who we are. Leonardo da Vinci, Gandhi, Susan B. Anthony and Oprah Winfrey have each embodied their prodigy, shared their gift and, as a result, realized an extraordinary level of self-actualization.

The prodigy within recognizes that by discovering your gift, sharing it through your ideal form of service and fulfilling your divine purpose—your calling—you begin to:

1. Truly believe in yourself, thus building the self-esteem necessary to tackle real change;

2. Recognize the extraordinary value you are generating and, based on this awareness, become motivated to confront and release the personal history, resentment (from not having been recognized and valued) and lifelong limitations (karmic patterns) that have held you back. In other words, it becomes easier to let go and pleasurably grow than to hold on, suffer, and never know who you could really be;

> *Pain transformed is expanded consciousness.*
>
> Luis Diaz

3. Finally know that it is your gift and giving that sustain you. As you continue to give from the prodigy you have within, you are sustained on an extraordinary level of synchronicity that supports every aspect of your life, and;

4. See, that over time, this process of living in alignment with the prodigy's Intentions results in the total transformation of your personality and the actualization of who you were born to be.

- The Prodigy Stories – Real life examples of the prodigy within.

Throughout most of the following chapters are Prodigy Stories. The Prodigy Stories are presented as illustrations of the Prodigy Principle they refer to. The stories range from my own very personal experiences to those of friends, clients and historical figures. Though most of the stories are fully factual narratives (in some cases the names have been changed), some are hybrids of several friends' or clients' experiences, while others are loosely based on true stories. In other words, they are part fiction to enhance the particular Prodigy Story at hand. The primary purpose of these stories is to bring a human face to the often theoretical information that precedes them. It is my hope that by reading these very human illustrations, you will gain a greater clarity, insight, and direction to assist you on the Quest to discover your calling.

- The Prodigy Practices – Recover your prodigy, cultivate accountability

At the end of each Prodigy Story is a reference to a Prodigy Practice. Though they are referenced in this book these 50 Practices are presented together in a workbook format, *The Prodigy Within Workbook.* Though the Prodigy Practices are not necessary to gaining a deeper relationship and communication with the prodigy within you, they have proved, for many, to be of considerable value. Each of the Practices represents a posture, attitude, or exercise designed to reveal, awaken, and liberate the prodigy within you. These Prodigy Practices are specifically designed to help you uncover the inner workings, dreams and goals of your prodigy within and to pinpoint your life's purpose. The exercise of these Practices purifies the mind/body of the impediments that have buried the prodigy in karmic patterns and kept it from being the vehicle for self-actualization that it is designed to be.

There are several ways to approach *The Prodigy Within Workbook*. I suggest that before you jump into the workbook, you finish reading The Prodigy Within or at least complete the chapter you are working with. By completing *The Prodigy Within* (or a chapter of the book), you will have acquainted yourself with the Principles (or individual principle) and given your mind time to integrate and present you with the requisite thoughts and feelings to better contemplate and complete the complementary Prodigy Practice.

How To Use *The Prodigy Within Workbook: The Prodigy Practices in the Workbook* should be approached with an open and playful attitude. The Practices will ask you to recall the passions, pastimes, and ambitions of your childhood; to review your current inspirations, habits and needs; and to define your dreams, hopes, and values for the future. They are best practiced somewhere you are comfortable to turn within. Somewhere you can turn off the outer world and sit in communion with your prodigy. Before actually writing your response to the question posed in each Prodigy Practice I suggest you ask the prodigy within for guidance and then take a contemplative moment to open your heart and mind to listen for your truth. In most cases I suggest being brief: spending one to five minutes on most will be more than adequate. If a Prodigy Practice inspires you to spend more time, definitely go for it. The purpose of these Practices is to reestablish your connection to the prodigy within you, attune your ear to its distinct voice, and activate your calling.

Prodigy Champions: Since many of the Prodigy Practices include a date, a time and a commitment, it is essential that you cultivate a form of accountability that works for you. I suggest generating one or more Prodigy Champions. These are people with whom you share a mutual respect, who are unabashedly committed to your success, who do not shame or chastise you, and who hold all that you share with them as sacred and secret. It is advantageous if they are already living their own calling or are as deeply committed as you are to discovering it. Over the course of reading the book and completing the Practices you will also come to recognize a wider circle of people that will represent your Prodigy Support System.

Once you have decided on your Prodigy Champion(s), you can structure your relationship so that you speak on the phone or in person anywhere from once a day to once a week for 15-30 minutes. During this time you will share the results of your Prodigy Practices, insights you've gained, and the Intentions that you have committed to accomplishing.

> *Life shrinks or expands in direct proportion to one's courage.*
>
> Anais Nin

To structure the conversation, there are four categories I use:

1. Practices and Insights: After reading a chapter or bulleted sub-category and doing the accompanying Practice, share your insights, lists, and revelations.

2. Define Your Intentions: Share the things you intend to do, and how and when you intend to do them. Make it simple. Practice brevity; it's often a key to taking responsibility, eliminating confusion, and avoiding failure.

3. What You Did or Didn't Accomplish: Describe how you did or did not fulfill your Intention, without going into a great deal of detail or generating an elaborate explanation. Remember, explanations are almost always the way we disguise excuses from ourselves.

4) Clarify and Re-State Your Intention: If you accomplished your Intention, you will briefly discuss what you learned and what you intend to do next. If you did not accomplish what you Intended,

tell your Prodigy Champion why you did not, any fears that arose that kept you from accomplishing the specific Intention, any clarity you obtained that dictated that you re-evaluate your Intention, and what you're going to change to accomplish it now. During this step, your Champion should ask supportive questions such as: "Why do you really want or need to do this?" "Is there some other way that you might accomplish this?" "Have you considered letting it go for now?" or "How can I assist you this time?"

Finally, before you get started reading *The Prodigy Within*, I would like to reiterate that most people enjoy the greatest success implementing the Principles in *The Prodigy Within* by reading through the entire book first and then going on to do The Prodigy Within Workbook.

- Heeding the Call – What Is a Calling and Where Do I Get One?

Our calling is the place where our gifts, skills, passions, and empathy meet the needs of the world. The Call arrives when we begin to recognize that we are not fulfilling our full potential and we have yet to make our contribution to the betterment of the world in which we live. Our worldview begins to shift from a place where, "I get my needs met," to a place where, "I fulfill my highest potential, and by doing so, I make a difference in the lives of others."

The idea that we arrive at a time in mid-life, where we make the shift from being self-centered to being of service to the world around us is a part of many cultural mythologies. The Hindu tradition dedicates the second half of life to spiritual pursuits; Buddha's commitment to the enlightenment of all sentient beings occurs halfway through his life; in Native American tradition, the elders are responsible for the spiritual well-being of the tribe; and in the Middle Ages, the myth of Parsifal's Search for the Holy Grail perfectly depicts how we transition from a self-centered life to the consciousness that asks the Question, "How may I be of service?"

The Call is activated as soon as an individual is ready to shift from "It's all about me" to "How may I be of service?" The specifics of our calling are revealed to us as we deepen the relationship with our prodigy. As the prodigy becomes the center of our life, we are guided to the specific visions, people, and opportunities where we can make a difference. Ultimately, benevolent intent—the way the universe miraculously supports us when we support ourselves—guides us to the interface between our talents, gifts, skills, interests, desires and the needs of the world that speak loudest to us.

> *The call rings up the curtain, always on a mystery of transfiguration … the time for passing the threshold is at hand.*
>
> *"The Hero of a Thousand Faces"*
>
> Joseph Campbell

Since what each of us has to offer is so different, we hear the Call through those skills, gifts, and talents that are uniquely ours. There are countless ways as to how the Call may be answered. For example, an executive manager with great organizational skills is guided to give one Saturday a month to establish a local Habitat for Humanity base. The preacher who's never found the right medium for his message hears the Call to make movies with an uplifting theme. Another person, gifted in carpentry but dissatisfied framing kitchens, is moved to make furniture out of recycled materials. A dress designer, with a store room full of "leftover" women's suits, collaborates with other designers to distribute business clothes to low-income women re-entering the work force. The ways to answer the Call are as many and varied as there are people.

For some, the Call may only require that they discover how to be more purposeful and positive in the life they are already living. If this is you, your prodigy may guide you to develop a new dimension to your work, or perhaps find a way make your workplace a more pleasant environment in which to spend eight hours a day. Your calling can be as simple as learning to smile everywhere you go. Nothing raises the vibration of a room, a business meeting, or those you come in daily contact with as powerfully as a positive attitude and a joyful smile. When I think of the Dalai Lama I don't think of what he does, I think of who he is, his infectious smile. This is what has endeared him to so many and made him an emissary of joy and peace.

Heeding the Call occurs when you hold the Intention to hear the prodigy's voice and then act on its guidance. When you have this commitment, you begin to generate a powerful, positive, prodigy-based momentum at the center of your life. It's important to remember that once you've decided to make a difference and ask the question, you have generated an Intention that will draw you to all you need to fulfill the prodigy's purpose. From this point on, it's important to pay attention to everything that shows up; sometimes the answer arrives in neon, but most of the time it arrives as quietly as a whisper, itch, or whim.

- Intention – What Is It and How Do I Make It Work For Me?

An Intention is defined as something that you plan to do or achieve, or the quality or state of having a purpose in mind. Intention is 1) the medium for transforming thought and desire into reality; 2) the architecture around which the physical and emotional levels of reality take form; and 3) the center of gravity that attracts to you all of the necessary elements, people, information, materials, and situations so that it will effortlessly manifest itself.

The importance of Intention cannot be stressed enough, not only in terms of discovering your calling, but also in every aspect of life where you have something that you would like to manifest. Whenever I start a project, consultation, or class, I invite those present to state their Intentions clearly before we begin. I remind them they went out of their way to create our time together, that they definitely came for something specific—conscious or unconscious—and that they must feel strongly about the likelihood we will manifest it or they probably wouldn't be willing to spend the time and money to receive it. I ask, "What exactly do you want to get out of this experience? What are you willing to do to make it happen?"

> *If I am not, who will I be?*
>
> Thoreau

When you state your Intention, it does not mean it will simply happen, but it does shift the responsibility upon you to do what it takes to manifest what you Intended—whether it be knowledge, an experience, a gift, or an opportunity. Once you have clearly stated your Intention and are acting in alignment with it, you need only remain open to what appears and trust the prodigy to guide you to take the appropriate action.

Just because you've generated an Intention doesn't mean you have to do everything that presents itself, that you have to be perfect or make it happen alone. Instead, seek the guidance of the prodigy within you and do what you are guided to do. That is all. The rest is done for you as a result of your actions and Intentions. Freed from playing God, you can enjoy the process of refining your Intuition, manifesting your Intention and observing the results.

The primary limitation to realizing your Intention is learning to identify your conscious and unconscious patterns and agendas that conflict with your stated Intention. When you've identified your conflicting Intentions, you 1) recognize them as they show up to undermine, seduce, and confuse you; 2) are able to release them; and 3) can re-commit yourself to your consciously stated Intention.

Because I wrote this book with the Intention that you discover your calling, but having no control over whether you do or not, the only way I can enhance the likelihood of it happening is to invite you, to generate a clear Intention before you begin. Obviously you sought out this book, expended energy and money to obtain it, and consciously or unconsciously had reason to believe it would be of value to you. It's likely that the title had meaning for you: *The Prodigy Within* The Quest to Discover Your Calling. If you chose this book because of the title, your Intention is already clear: "By reading this book, I will discover my calling." If that is the case, make it your spoken Intention to do whatever it takes to discover your true calling. What do you want out of it? What do you hope to receive? What level of participation are you willing to take responsibility for? Are you willing to generate an Intention to discover your calling and do what you feel, hear, and sense is necessary to harness the unfolding of this Intention? It is up to you not to let this book turn into just another self-help book that did not fulfill your expectations.

> *It has been wisely said that people get in trouble in this life not because they want too much but because they settle for too little.*
>
> *"How to Find the Work You Love"*

Once you are clear that you are reading this book to discover and live your calling, it will be much easier and far more pleasurable to embrace every aspect of the process. Casually reading the book as though that were enough and avoiding the deeply reflective processes inherent in the Prodigy Practices will limit the value you receive and the likelihood of manifesting your Intention. That doesn't mean you have to do every Prodigy Practice or do them all perfectly; it means you should do what your prodigy guides you to do to fulfill your Intention. For example, there are over 50 Prodigy Practices throughout the book designed to assist you in revealing, liberating, and embracing your prodigy. You don't need to do every one of them. Some will speak to you, some will seem obvious, some ludicrous and still others useless. Some may only inspire a word or a sentence while others will generate an avalanche of memories, feelings, and revelations. Embracing the Prodigy Practices that speak to you or challenge you will transform them from a chore into an enlightening adventure. You need only show up with the Intention that your prodigy guide you and that your heartfelt efforts will generate the clarity, guidance, and inspiration you need to reveal your purpose. Before you go any further, decide on your Intention.

Prodigy Practice #1 - Your Intention: State Your Intention for reading The Prodigy Within

1) Define your Intention for buying, reading, and using this book. Make it simple and straightforward. State it in the first person. A clearly and precisely stated intention will result in your receiving precisely what you want and need: an enlightening, uplifting, and empowering directive. If you have any patterns, beliefs or agendas that conflict with your Intention, briefly state them and create an Intention to recognize and release them as they arise.

2) Create the intention to discover your Calling. Before you go any further in the book, ask the prodigy within, "How may I be of service?" It's important to remember that the answer doesn't have to be monumental. Your form of service may be to make peoples lives easier, more pleasurable, or more fun. That is, in itself, enough. Af-

ter a moment of meditation where you consciously Intend to receive guidance, write down any images, thoughts, or feelings that arise. Remember there's no right answer, only the opportunity to open the channel for the prodigy within to begin speaking to you through insights, inspiration, and attraction. It may be helpful to use the following questions as a guide:

1. What can I do to make a difference today?
2. Where do I experience the greatest joy?
3. What simple thing can I begin to do to make my world a better place?
4. Where would I like to make a difference in the future?
5. What, in the world, could benefit from my energy, talents, and commitment?

PART II

THE 7 PRINCIPLES OF PRODIGY

A Manual for Discovering and Developing the Prodigy Within

CHAPTER 3

Principle #1: SUMMON THE COURAGE TO *WANT*

Prodigies know who they are and exactly what they want. Their entire world revolves around developing their gift. They are possessed by a childlike sense of wonder, passion, and enthusiasm. They have, to an extraordinary degree, a sense of their calling and the courage to want, above all else, to fulfill it.

So where does that leave the rest of us? Maybe you're among those who have tried every door and every angle you could think of but still don't know exactly what you want in life (or what you want to be when you grow up). Perhaps you know what you want, but you've been unable to manifest it and it has dissipated into simply hoping and wishing. Or maybe you've reached the point where you've given up wanting and begun to believe that "it'll never happen." Don't worry; chances are you're much closer than you think. In fact, the primary premise of this book is that even if you feel that you've lost all contact with the prodigy within you, it has never stopped guiding you toward fulfilling your destiny.

This chapter is designed to re-establish your connection to the prodigy within you, define what you want, and empower you to burn with focus, passion, and want once again. In this chapter you will:

> *Genuis is nothing more or less than childhood recovered ... a childhood now equipped for self-expression with an adult's capacities.*
>
> Charles Baudelaire

1) Rediscover the interests, dreams, and passions that time and distance have extinguished.

2) Recognize that lost years (time spent doing things that seemed off track) were not lost, but a time of research and preparation.

3) Acknowledge the excuses you've created to distract you from your heart's true calling.

4) Clarify your destination, chart a preliminary course of action and, above all, reconnect with your wants, charged with the conviction that you will attain them.

- When I Grow Up

When children are asked what they want to be when they grow up, they talk about things that seem important to adults like a "doctor, president, or teacher," while they may boast to their friends about becoming a "movie star, athlete, or zillionaire." Of course, most children don't know what they want to be when they grow up; they just know what they love to do now. If they are among the fortunate ones who have parents or mentors that support their passions, they are far more likely to develop their talents or interests into a meaningful vocation and, ultimately, their calling. This does not mean that if you did not receive adequate support, you are doomed to never realize your true gifts; it is likely, though, that your confidence, intuition, and perseverance were adversely affected. If you never received the encouragement you needed to "go for it," you probably learned to settle for a great deal less than you deserve. When you learn to settle, your gifts never become more than a pastime or hobby—or you abandon them altogether to earn a living and be responsible. If all this has left you feeling frustrated or hopeless, take a breath—you can still revive the prodigy within and discover your calling.

> *When I approach a child, he inspires in me two sentiments; tenderness for what he is, and respect for what he may become.*
>
> Louis Pasteur

You can accomplish this by 1) revisiting your childhood, recovering your dreams, and remembering what you loved to do when left to your own devices; 2) forgiving your parents and others for not supporting and nurturing your gifts; 3) committing to be there for yourself; and 4) summoning the desire to re-ignite your childhood wonder and passion.

Prodigy Story:

I met Joshua when he was 12 years old. I was volunteering at a school that was based on the English experimental school, Summerhill. The philosophy of the school was that, when children were deeply involved in pursuing their innate passions, they would find their way to a well-rounded education as a means to extend their knowledge deeper into their passion. Joshua might as well have been the poster child for the school. At the ripe old age of 12, Joshua knew more about insects than any person I've ever met. He was so passionate about the creatures that he was learning Latin to understand the root derivations of their names. In order to read the various scientific journals that his mother bought him, Joshua had taught himself to read at a high school level. In addition he studied chemistry, math, and art to extend his knowledge into ever-broadening arenas. Joshua already knew what some of us never learn: the more he indulged his interest, the more opportunities he created to do what he loved.

Because Joshua received unwavering support from his family and committed to his passion for entomology at such a young age, he blazed a direct path to his calling. Joshua is now an adult and an authority on rare tropical insects. His passion for insects has led him to become an environmental activist protecting the ecological environments of these rare and beautiful beings. As when he was a child, Joshua's love for insects has not narrowed his interests or confined him to living life with blinders on; to the contrary, Joshua continues to expand his gift by studying international law to help protect their habitats while pursuing every opportunity to speak about the role his "friends" play in the health and longevity of our planet.

Prodigy Practice #2 – Sifting for Clues: Childhood passions, hobbies, and pastimes.

- Love It, Want It, Do It!

Knowing what you love to do is an essential prerequisite of wanting to do it. As soon as we want, we begin to conceive of ways to get it. Wanting naturally evolves into doing; doing, in turn, gets us deeper in touch with our wanting. If what we are doing doesn't feel good, then that will indicate it is not a viable guide to our calling. If the things we are doing have real meaning and energy for us, then we will want to do them more.

> *In my imagination I constantly reenacted heroic episodes, and I was always the hero.*
>
> Sir Edmond Hillary

We must all recall what we love and have loved since childhood. If you're not in touch with what you love doing it may be because you've abandoned it so often that you're afraid to feel it again. Always choosing the adult thing to do, sacrificing a fuller life to earn more money, and always doing what you think you have to do over what you want to do all contribute to losing touch with our passions. Over time, an emotional wasteland results. It is important to recognize the story we tell ourselves about why we are not doing what we love. That story is a Great Wall of China, separating a life of struggle from a life of joy and bounty. Once we are doing what we love, the wasteland is transformed; the land bears fruit and our world is resurrected.

What do you love? Left to your own devices, what would you do with your free time? If you didn't have to earn a living and had the money to set yourself up in a field, hobby, or project that ignites your fire, what would it be? It's essential at this point in your Quest to be clear about what you love. Following what you love to do will guide you in your Quest to discover your calling.

Prodigy Story:

Monica's story demonstrates the serendipitous way life unfolds when we pursue what we love. Monica's favorite thing to do when she was a little girl was to design and build furniture. She filled journals with drawings of furniture and redesigned and rebuilt each of her store-bought dollhouses. She remembers the day she gave up her passion:

> *Look at life with the eyes of a child.*
>
> Henri Matisse

It was her mother's birthday and a party was planned for that evening. While her mother was at the beauty parlor, Monica rearranged the living room as a surprise gift. She first made drawings, then moved the furniture, and finally arranged the various knick-knacks. When Monica's mother came home that afternoon, stressed from running around all day, rather than praising Monica's efforts, she lost control and began ranting. Monica recalls, "Something in me died that day." From that time forward, Monica stopped building furniture, began to give up her "tomboy ways" and later, at her mother's prompting, sought a legitimate profession that would offer her a lifetime of security. Monica sacrificed her greatest source of joy and all hope of ever doing what she loved.

At 38 years of age, Monica, now an accountant, felt stuck doing something she hated and found herself resentful of people who had discovered their calling. Not wanting to live a life of bitterness and regret, Monica began to reawaken her passion for furniture and interior design. When she felt the familiar but long-lost stirrings coming back to life, she proclaimed her Intention: "Even if I starve to death, I'm never going to do work I don't love again." With that decision, Monica took a job at a furniture store and began making and selling exotic, brightly colored end tables. The work barely paid the bills, but she kept at it.

The owner of the store loved Monica's playful end tables, purchased several, and invited Monica to design the front window of the store around them. Soon she was selling two or three every month out of the store window. When a couple who had purchased one of the end tables discovered that Monica had made it, they invited her to come to their home after work and help them with some decorating ideas. It wasn't long before word spread about Monica's innate design sense, and soon the store was booking her for design consultations. After a couple of consultations, Monica knew that she had at last found her calling.

> *I am convinced all of humanity is born with more gifts than we know. Most are born geniuses and just get de-geniused rapidly.*
>
> R. Buckminster Fuller

While she continued to work at the furniture store and build her business, Monica decided it was time to go back to school and learn everything she could about design. After a couple years, she got her degree and has since built a successful interior design business. Today Monica is highly regarded for her unique style and has expanded her end table business into an exotic and playful, one-of-a-kind furniture line.

Prodigy Practice #3 – Love: Lost & Found: Things you've loved and abandoned.

- Useful Folly – The Lost Years Were Not Lost

Throughout our lives, as we stumble through brain-numbing jobs, bad relationships, and a wide array of successes and failures, the prodigy within us has always played a role—sometimes as lead, sometimes supporting—in steering us toward our full potential. As we undertake the process of reflecting on the seemingly haphazard path our lives have taken, the overarching guidance of the prodigy will become apparent. Periods of life that previously appeared chaotic, dictated by necessity, or that ended in failure will be seen anew as necessary steps on the path toward preparing to embrace our calling. The years spent wandering in the wilderness are recognized as a time spent gathering tools, developing and mastering skills, and ultimately preparing the way for the prodigy to step to center stage. When you acknowledge the value of the Lost Years you 1) deepen the process of forgiving yourself and your caretakers; 2) sharpen the focus on your passions, gifts, and wants; and 3) re-establish a loving dialogue with your prodigy within. You will also inadvertently begin to release feelings of shame, denial, or perfectionism that may have unconsciously paralyzed you. Releasing these feelings frees up an enormous storehouse of energy that often times catapults us toward fulfilling our highest aspirations.

> *Lord, grant that I may always desire more than I accomplish.*
>
> Michelangelo

Prodigy Story:

The story of Sandra illustrates how years you may have thought were lost to useless pursuits are not lost at all; they are simply another way the prodigy guides you to your calling.

Sandra was devastated when her husband left her with two young children and no means of support. Trained as a nurse, she had not worked for over ten years. When Sandra and I began talking, I asked her about the things she had done in her life that brought her the greatest joy and satisfaction—when did she feel the most purposeful? Without blinking Sandra began speaking passionately about writing and researching her master's thesis on the positive role of elders in primitive societies. She became dewy eyed when she recalled how good she felt interviewing and working with them. She spoke of how she loved listening to their stories and how they showered her with love and acceptance. We decided that, to get back in touch with that aspect of herself, she should volunteer at a retirement home once a week. That's all it took.

After six months of working with the elderly, she was clear this is where she was always meant to be. Sandra felt, even though she didn't know it at the time, all her previous jobs, her education, and the years spent raising children were preparation for this moment. Within a year she bought her first retirement home.

Sandra now says she wakes up every day feeling truly blessed. Though she's fully aware of the positive impact she has on so many lives, she, like so many others who have discovered their calling, feels she is receiving far more than she is giving.

Prodigy Practice #4 – Inventory of Experiences: Jobs, projects & dreams.

- Peak Experiences

As humans, perhaps the most inspiring moments we ever have fall into the category of peak experiences. Abraham Maslow, the humanistic psychologist, defined peak experiences as "any experience in which an individual feels totally alive, hyper-aware, in unity with all life and, upon completion, unquestionably transformed."

In Maslow's groundbreaking research into the phenomena of peak experiences, he discovered that self-actualized people were far more likely to have peak experiences than those who are overly concerned with responsibility, rational explanations, and "earning a living." Though what exactly triggers peak experiences remains a mystery, we do know that those who are passionate about their lives and work are far more likely to have them.

In interviewing and reading autobiographies of prodigies, I was initially astounded to hear how often they spoke of peak experiences when referring to their work and their lives. This being the case, identifying the peak experiences we've had could serve as a powerful trigger to reawaken our passions and to indicate the direction of our gift and calling. My research indicates peak experiences represent a time when the prodigy surfaced in our life, fully awake, active and taking the leadership role it was designed for. I have had numerous peak experiences in my own life; some had to do with my calling, others with exceeding my own limited perception of my capabilities.

> *Internal voices that have been muted for years clamour to be heard.*
>
> Daniel Levinson,

When I was twelve years old, I was in the state championships in gymnastics. While sitting on the sidelines waiting for my turn at one competition, I watched as one competitor after another did routines that were far more complicated and demanding than what I was planning to do. As I sat there, something in me shifted; I mentally stepped out of my self-imposed limitations into a place of knowing that anything was possible. I made a decision at that moment that I would do the tricks the others were doing, even though I'd never done them before. When my turn came, I approached the parallel bars in what I can only describe as an altered state. Without thinking, I launched into a routine at a level of difficulty and complexity I'd never before attempted. When it was over, the crowd cheered riotously, my coach embraced me with joyous disbelief, and the judges rewarded me with third place. From that day forward, I was changed forever. Since then I have had a number of similar peak experiences in "high pressure" moments, all with the belief that I was capable of miraculous things.

Prodigy Story:

Jerry went to film school in the 70s with dreams of becoming a documentary filmmaker. School was a great experience for Jerry. He loved everything about making films: the collaboration, the creativity, the opportunity to "make a difference." Fresh out of film school, Jerry was hired by a cable TV station to produce his first documentary. His elation at the opportunity, however, soon dissolved into frustration. As every filmmaker learns sooner or later, the entertainment industry is fickle. After running into endless red tape and roadblocks, Jerry's frustration finally turned into annihilation. The film never got made. Jerry left his passion, his gift, and peak experiences behind. Twenty-five years later, when we began to work together, Jerry didn't even bother to include filmmaking as one of his loves. When we finally stumbled on his hastily buried dream of becoming a filmmaker, Jerry was in complete denial of how much it meant to him. But once he finally uncovered the topic, Jerry began waxing poetic about those heady days he experienced as a filmmaker. To hear him recall that time in his life, one would believe that all he experienced every day was a continuous stream of peak experiences: the first time the camera rolled, an actor delivered a transcendent performance and the entire crew shared a peak experience right there on the set; spending three days and three nights straight editing his graduate film; arguing, creating, and collaborating with his team while slamming down coffee and devouring pancakes at 4:00 a.m.; being lifted out of his day to day existence "into another sweeter more exciting world" as he wrote for fourteen straight hours for weeks on end.

As Jerry became liberated from the tangled web of painful memories, he discovered his core values and recognized the prodigy within's joy when he was making films; there was no doubt in his mind what he wanted to do with his life. Today Jerry has returned to his passion for filmmaking, loves what he's doing, and reports that he is once again enjoying the inspiring presence of peak experiences in his life and work.

Prodigy Practice #5 – Peak Experiences: Extraordinary moments in your life.

- Wanting

As children, we are big bundles of wants. Some we get, others we don't. Some wants are actually necessities; others are indulgences. For most of us, the very idea of wanting is charged with an incendiary list of feelings and memories. For some, wanting equates with being selfish; for others, wanting is avoided for fear of failing. For still others, it is a long and shame-filled list of bad choices; weakness, unworthiness, self denial—you name it. Yes, they are all excuses and we all have them. In order to recover your courage to want, you must acknowledge what has come between you and your wants and develop a conscious, intuitive, and pro-active means to honor wanting.

Prodigy Story:

Audrey had given up wanting anything. She had adopted the attitude that she could never have what she wanted so why even want anymore? She was paralyzed by the regrets she had been carrying for years because she had to discontinue her graduate studies to care for her sick father. Over time, she gave up all the things she loved to do and settled into a life of silent desperation. She felt sentenced to a life without dreams, hope, or direction—a life of settling and just getting by.

> *How often I found where I should be going by setting out for somewhere else.*
>
> R. Buckminster Fuller

When we first spoke, Audrey said that the only place in her life she felt any real satisfaction was when she was standing around the water cooler, leaning over a co-worker's desk or meeting with friends over coffee to help them sort through their feelings. As she spoke, she realized the depth of her pain and the fact that, not only had she given up wanting more from life, she'd also given up any hope of ever finding and doing what she loved. As we began to process the full scope of Audrey's feelings regarding who she is and what she's "supposed to be doing," she became willing to entertain the idea that there might be some other way to re-ignite her dream of helping others.

When a friend suggested that the endless hours spent coaching, supporting, and commiserating with friends and co-workers might be the precise education required for an advice columnist, Audrey lit up. Her friend lovingly reminded her she already had the equivalent of a master's degree in doing what she loved and needed only to find additional ways to share her gift. As the light shined onto what had been her sense of hopelessness, Audrey began to dare to dream and want again. Once she was willing to admit to wanting it, she came up with a plan to make it happen. Within weeks, Audrey was writing an advice column for a local throwaway newspaper.

As so often happens, one positive, consciously taken step in the direction of our calling begets another. Audrey's column grew, spread to a couple of other local papers, and then expanded into a local cable TV show. Audrey, who is currently negotiating a number of opportunities, admits that even if they don't come together, she feels like the "luckiest girl alive." Now that she is no longer afraid to want, Audrey's created extensive lists of her long- and short-term wants that include everything from a book deal to learning to scuba dive.

> *Eminent people whose lives present the most striking examples of calling are characterized by ... by one supreme factor ... motivation.*
>
> *"The Soul's Code"*
>
> *James Hillman*

Prodigy Practice #6 – I Want To: Create a list of your prodigy's wants.

- There's No Excuse for Excuses - Explanations, Rationalizations or Justifications.

Can you imagine Van Gogh having difficulty finding time to paint? What if Mozart couldn't afford the "right" piano to practice on? Would Einstein have held off on his research while waiting to receive a grant? Think about anything you've really wanted—haven't you always found a way to make it happen or had a really good excuse why it couldn't?

The admonition to summon The Courage to Want will never

have any meaning or power to change your life if your first response to wanting is making excuses. I define excuses as any explanation given to avoid doing what you want or know that you should do. That doesn't mean that every explanation is an excuse. If, however, you're not clear about what you want, it might be valuable to listen to yourself the next time you offer an explanation. When you observe yourself making excuses, examine your motivations. Are you afraid that what you want is beyond your reach? Do you hedge your bets by rationalizing that it's not really that important anyway? Do you justify your considerations by blaming an ego run amok? As you relinquish your dependence on excuses, explanations, considerations, rationalizations, and justifications, you 1) rehabilitate your trust in the prodigy within; 2) erode the old pattern of fear; 3) create a healthy relationship between wanting and doing; 4) generate positive feedback; and 5) ground the Courage to Want.

Prodigy Story:

Lauren's story demonstrates what can happen when we stop making excuses. When Lauren and I first met, she was a therapist with a floundering practice and a million legitimate excuses for not following her calling. Though Lauren was clear that being a therapist was her calling, she had reached a place where she felt there was no way she could actualize it. She spoke in depth about the pain she experienced watching her practice disintegrate, her feeling that she was failing her clients, and hopelessness of ever finding a solution to her dilemma that wouldn't cost her her therapist's license.

Lauren wanted to include the Tarot cards in her therapy sessions, but believed she would be judged and censured by her peers and the Licensing Board. Lauren made an extensive list of excuses as to why she couldn't include Tarot in her practice. One by one we discussed every excuse. Many of her excuses crumbled as we spoke about them;

for those excuses that were legitimate, we created an action plan for discovering a solution or a viable alternative. Over the next several months Lauren systematically dealt with every excuse she had come up with. As she processed her excuses, opportunities to do Tarotpy (Tarot-based therapy) began to appear out of nowhere: a local bookstore owner, who normally only invited authors of new books to speak there, asked Lauren to do a three week class on Tarotpy; soon after, Lauren's former mentor went to bat for her, landing a speaking engagement and workshop on the Tarot at a highly prestigious professional conference. Excuses continued to dissipate as Lauren began to realize that she had something of tremendous value to offer.

> *If we did all the things we were capable of, we would astound ourselves.*
>
> Thomas A. Edison

Today Lauren has a thriving practice that features the Tarot, teaches workshops in Tarotpy, has been interviewed by numerous lay and professional magazines, and was just hired to train future psychologists, at the graduate school level, in the use of Tarot as a therapeutic tool.

Prodigy Practice #7a – Dirty Laundry: An inventory of excuses to avoid doing.

Prodigy Practice #7b – Excusing Excuses: Create an embargo on excuses.

- *Just Do It*

Buddhists believe there are only two basic motivations in life: moving toward pleasure or moving away from pain. Think about it, whether you're eating, exercising, dating, or working, you're either looking for ways to increase your pleasurable experiences or avoid the painful ones. Whether you're on a diet, disciplining your child, or 50 minutes into a grueling workout, you have to find a way to make it pleasurable or you'd remove yourself from the pain of it. The diet has to make you thinner, the discipline has to help your child get into college, and the exercise regime must give you more energy and make you feel better. An action initially perceived as unpleasurable becomes considerably more pleasurable when you know it will help you realize an important goal.

When I look at my greatest accomplishments, I find that most of them required doing a lot of things I didn't want to do and didn't think I'd enjoy doing. When I now consider going after something I want, I always ask myself if it's worth "the price of admission." In other words, will the outcome—the pleasurable payoff I'm hoping for—be worth the pain or discomfort I'll have to go through to make it happen? After years of approaching my wants in this way, I now actually get pleasure from situations I used to define as painful. In fact, by remaining aware of the payoff and grateful to be growing into the person you know you are meant to be, every challenging situation can be perceived and embraced as a wonderful opportunity.

Of course, even when we let go of our excuses and learn to enjoy the journey, attaining wants we feel strongly about remains challenging. Know that without passion and fearlessness you will find there is "never enough time" (or energy or resources) to fulfill your prodigy's wants. By committing to your dream, cultivating divine selfishness, and maintaining an "attitude of gratitude," you can begin to build the unstoppable momentum required to manifest your dreams and calling. Bottom line, it's time to give up your laundry list of excuses and Just Do It.

Prodigy Story:

For the last 20 years, Donald had been working in a job where he felt trapped. In the last several years, he found himself obsessing about returning to college to revisit his long-abandoned dream of being a psychologist. Every time Donald considered making the change, he came up with a hundred excuses why he shouldn't or couldn't. He wrote out lists of pros and cons and, though he felt the reasons on the pro side were substantial, he was never able to come to terms with the issues on the con side: "My family's grown used to the lifestyle my excellent salary affords us;" "My wife loves staying home and caring for the children;" "I'm too old to go back to school for four years;" "I can't figure out how to work for nothing for a year while I'm accumulating the 3,000 hours I'll need to get my license;" "My accountant told me if I just keep working for twelve more years I'll have enough to retire at 68 if we scale back a little." Every excuse confirmed he'd have to bite the bullet, "do the right thing" for his family, and put away his foolish dream. Every time Donald and I talked his list was longer, the excuses more convincing and his frustration escalating. He worked very hard to convince himself his dream was frivolous, his responsibilities overwhelming, and potential solutions were virtually non-existent.

> *It is when I am, as it were, completely myself, entirely alone, and of good cheer … that ideas flow best and most abundantly. Whence and how they come, I know not, nor can I force them.*

I asked Donald to imagine himself sitting in his office, assisting his therapy clients through their issues. Then I asked him to describe what that was like. As he spoke about the feelings of joy and satisfaction he felt helping these people, he began to cry. When he realized how deeply he had buried his need to help others and how incredible it would feel to finally be doing it, he realized he had to Just Do It or "shrivel up and pack it in."

So often all it takes to turn things around is taking the first step. I suggested that Donald just start doing the things he could, without making huge commitments or sacrifices. For Donald, the first step was to get his ancient college transcripts and look into schools that had nighttime, weekend, and Internet classes. Once he discovered a college that accepted his existing college credits and had nighttime and weekend classes, all of Donald's excuses began to miraculously resolve themselves. His wife suddenly became excited about going back to work in the field she loved; another company, similar to the one he worked for, offered him part-time work—and a 25% raise—that could be done on his own schedule; and, much to his delight, there were many students older than Donald in all of his classes.

Once Donald began listening to the prodigy within, everything seemed to fall into place. He is finally doing what he dreamt about for years and, according to Donald, his quality of life has improved in every area: he loves school; he's enjoying his "Mr. Mom" role and watching his children grow up; the long-standing strain on his marriage has evaporated; and he is ecstatic that he is finally being true to himself and responsible to his family.

Prodigy Practice #8 — Do It Now! What have you avoided doing?

CHAPTER 4

Principle #2:
EXPECT THE BEST

Prodigies believe wholeheartedly in their gifts and their abilities. They not only expect the best, they expect to be the best. They are possessed by an unquenchable need to excel and will go to any lengths to do so. They are motivated by a powerful sense of mission and, even as neophytes, are legends in their own minds. In anything pertaining to their gift, prodigies view excesses as assets. They consider a degree of obsession as essential to becoming the best.

For many of us, going for what we want is land-mined with feelings, feelings of not being deserving, not being good enough, not expecting the best. If you find yourself having trouble expecting the best, you might want to ask yourself if you 1) set realistic goals; 2) work with a focused commitment to achieve those goals; and 3) accept the outcome without self-criticism or comparison. When we set a realistic goal, achieve it (at or near the level of expectation), and accept the outcome, we re-educate ourselves to expect the best. If you did not receive this wisdom from your parents or a mentor, then it's time to parent the prodigy within you.

- Parenting the Prodigy Within

One of the main things that distinguishes those who find their calling at a young age from those who spend years seeking and developing it is often a parent, teacher, or mentor who recognizes the prodigy within the child and goes about guiding, supporting, and inspiring the child to follow its lead. More often than not, the children of these kinds of parents learn to expect the best—rather than fear the worst—because of the consistent support and guidance they receive. They learn to jump in; knowing that if they falter their parents will be there to help them through.

So often one hears stories of athletes, musicians, and dedicated students whose parents sacrificed everything for them to develop their gift. These parents think nothing of driving their child to practice every day at the ice rink; installing a basketball court for daily drills; hiring coaches, tutors, and trainers; working extra hours to make sure there's enough money for the right school, the next competition, and the very best equipment; and even packing up the house and moving if there's a better location in which to nurture their prodigy. You probably knew people like this when you were growing up. Their parents went out of their way to help them, never missed a game, checked their homework every night, and dedicated themselves to their child's calling. Mozart's father was a highly regarded piano teacher who gave his son every opportunity to develop his talent. He personally traveled all over Europe with him so the young Mozart could perfect his playing, perform before a wide array of audiences, and compose music for every possible occasion.

As adults, those of us who didn't receive this kind of continuous love, support, and sacrifice are often painfully aware of how the absence of it manifests in our lives as caution, fear, consideration, low self-esteem, poor self-image, and all the other ways we find ourselves unable consistently to expect the best. So what do we do? No, not hate our parents. Rather we learn, as adults, to parent our own prodigy within. Where do we start? We start by taking a good, honest look at whether or not we treat ourselves, our dreams, our talents, and our need to discover our calling with the same quality of love, guidance, and direction we would offer our own child.

> *I'd asked ten or fifteen people for suggestions. Finally one lady friend asked the right question. "Well, what do you love most?" That's how I started painting money.*
>
> Andy Warhol

An infant bangs on the side of her bed for hours at a time. One parent, frazzled and frustrated yells at the child to "stop that racket," while another parent pads the side of the crib and buys drumsticks for the child. You need to ask yourself what you would do. How can you support your prodigy to assist in navigating you toward your calling? Even if you don't know what your calling is, you can still parent your prodigy by affording yourself every opportunity to explore, play, practice, and seek. You can learn to coach, console, and inspire yourself to stick with it, have patience, and show up the best you can. You can observe the ways you practice the same belittling, shaming, and unsupportive behavior you may have learned as a child when you fell short of the mark or the expectations your parents expressed. Just as when you're tired you make sure you get rest and when you're sad you treat yourself with loving kindness, when you're lost it helps to seek guidance from a friend or professional who might be a little farther along the path. It's up to us to create the most perfect physical, mental, emotional and spiritual environment that we can for our prodigy to at last take the reins and lead us to our destiny.

Prodigy Story:

At six months of age, Tiger Woods preferred to go without dinner than miss sitting in his high chair watching his father drive golf balls into a net. When other children were practicing walking, Tiger, under the watchful eye of his father, was tirelessly practicing his swing. When he was two, he won his first tournament. At five, he appeared on the television show "That's Incredible." At eight, he won the Junior World ten-and-under division. At twelve, he broke 70, a feat most adults never accomplish. Even with all of his natural talent and early success, it was his parents' guidance and unqualified support that conditioned Tiger to expect the best and to become the best. Tiger's parents taught him there's no such thing as failure, only opportunities to learn, practice more, grow and then, having done all he could, to expect the best. They taught him to put his anger and disappointment to work, not by dwelling on his failures or judging himself mercilessly, but by hunkering down, creating a plan, and trying again. They taught him about the futility of comparing himself to others. They used Tiger's intense focus on playing, competing, and striving for perfection to teach him the values and integrity of balancing his extraordinary achievements with humility and compassion for himself and others.

In reading about Tiger's younger years, three themes stand out regarding his parents' exemplary commitment to the prodigy within their son. They taught him to 1) balance his enormous dreams with challenging and realistic goals; 2) maintain balance between hard work and the rest of his life: school, friends, hobbies, and other sports; and 3) accept the outcome of every game. They always confirmed to him that he had done his best, that losing a game didn't mean he was a failure, and that his weaknesses, with work, would become strengths. His parents' love and unqualified support gave Tiger the confidence to expect the best, which in Tiger's case included supplying the work ethic and determination to be the best. As we learn to parent our own prodigy within, it is a foregone conclusion that we will come to expect the best while taking an enormous step toward becoming the best.

Prodigy Practice #9 – Parenting the Prodigy Within: Balance love, discipline & support.

• Core Beliefs – "Seed Thought" or Organizing Core Myth the Self is Built Around

The themes and messages internalized from childhood that constitute how we feel about ourselves are held in place by a core belief. We all have a number of core beliefs, but here we will deal with the one that defines our relationship to giving, doing, and being in the world. This core belief is the infrastructure around which we build our concept of self and our beliefs regarding what we are capable of. Until the beams, posts, and girders that make up the architecture of our core belief are identified, we cannot begin to live our calling. How can we expect the best if we believe the worst? Prodigies like Tiger Woods who were lucky enough to have parents, teachers, and mentors who imparted to them a positive and uplifting core belief definitely have an advantage. For example, the core belief that someone like Tiger might have internalized could be summed up by any or all of the following: "You're great; failures are growth opportunities; we love you no matter what; we believe you will fulfill all of your dreams." Wow! What a cool place to begin your life's journey. Though this kind of internalized core belief doesn't make you immune to losing your way, it certainly grounds you firmly on your path.

> *Hold yourself responsible for a higher standard than anyone else expects of you. Never excuse yourself.*
>
> Henry Ward Beecher

At the other end of the spectrum you might have internalized a less than supportive core belief like the one I received: "You might be a genius but nothing you ever do will be good enough." This core belief effectively instilled in me the belief that I would always fall short of my goals, that my supposed intelligence was useless and that I was unworthy of love. Every time I took on a career challenge that resulted in a success, it would inevitably be followed by turmoil and then a degree of failure. Although the turmoil took on many forms, it consistently resulted in the confirmation of my core belief. I somehow managed to find a way, in every experience, success, or failure, ultimately to prove the truth of my core belief that "Nothing I ever do will be good enough." Over time this resulted in the debilitating feeling, "Why even bother trying?"

The negative core beliefs around which each of us builds our self-concept take a wide variety of forms. It's my experience that each of our core beliefs is held internally in a precise structure of words and sentences; these may have been originally spoken by a parent or communicated silently through their actions. No matter how you acquired your core belief, what's important is that you discover it exactly as you have internalized it. When you've identified your core belief, the tumblers begin to fall into place, unlocking the unconscious and revealing your worldview, as though for the first time, as an extension and expression of this belief. Though I knew for years the generally karmic pattern I was living out, it wasn't until my precise core belief was revealed that I began to find freedom from the painful pattern in which I felt hopelessly trapped.

The following are some of the various core beliefs I have come across in my coaching and consulting. As you read these, it will be painfully obvious how destructive, devastating, and demoralizing unconscious internalized core beliefs can be:

- "It's not okay for me to be (totally) happy."
- "No matter what I do, I'm not seen for who I am."
- "Why bother doing anything? You'll never make a difference. The darkness will win and you'll be annihilated."
- "I'm only a visitor. I don't belong here. I'll never amount to anything. What's the use?"
- "Just when I think I'm going to succeed, something happens and I don't."

Prodigy Story:

David, a client with whom I had been working for years, is an excellent example of the freedom that comes from the revelation of one's unconscious and destructive core belief. Though David had done a great deal of therapy and self-searching, over the years he remained locked in a cycle that always left him feeling diminished, alone, and unacknowledged. After banging up against this pattern again and again in the course of our work together, I suggested that maybe he had a core belief that was overpowering and undermining the clearly stated intentions we were creating. David's willingness to look inside revealed the true devil in the machine; he realized he had internalized his father's unspoken message to him as a core belief: "You're not important. You have to take care of yourself or no one will. Don't ever expect me to be there for you, my life is much more important than yours." Based on his core belief David always ended up taking on more than he should, working with people who didn't value him and falling short of his (and their) unrealistic goals.

David translated this belief into a feeling of worthlessness, that no matter how hard he tried he'd never get his needs met or obtain his most cherished dreams. As an adult, every project or business David undertook confirmed his internalized core belief. When David finally identified his core belief, faced it in all of its previous iterations, allowed himself the feelings of anger, sadness, and frustration that accompanied it, and rewrote it in words, deeds, and awareness; his calling came into a clear focus and his life's work took an enormous leap forward. David narrowed his focus to working with children and adults with brain trauma and learning disabilities. He took a job at a clinic where, even though he was initially under-appreciated, he came to be seen and valued by the lead M.D. and patients as a truly gifted healer. David's core belief began to disintegrate as he was acknowledged daily for his extraordinary gift, found his way back into a PhD program (he had fled years before as proof of his unworthiness), and generated a community of individuals who support and believe in him unequivocally. For the first time in his life David feels he is taking care of himself and the world is providing what he needs to do so. David's forming a new core belief that is the result of the reality he is generating by his courageous and unwavering commitment to his prodigy and to unfolding his calling.

My life is important. What I have to give is an important part of the dance of life.

Prodigy Practice #10 – Core Belief: Rewrite your internalized message of defeat.

• Clean Your House – Remove Yourself from Toxic Situations—Eliminate Toxic People

It's hard to expect the best when the people around you expect the worst and feel it's their duty to play "devil's advocate," remind you of all the things that could possibly go wrong, question whether you've considered "your responsibilities," or insinuate that you're "losing touch with reality." If you have people like this in your life and consider them friends, it's time to reconsider the meaning of friendship. In case the definition of "friend" has become blurred over time, it's something like, someone you have a close, personal relationship with which is based on mutual trust and affection; someone who supports, defends, and believes in you.

The strength and courage it takes to step forth and deliver our gift to the world is nothing short of monumental. Critical to our success is creating a safe place (home, family and support) for our adult prodigy to grow, develop confidence, and build momentum. Sam Keen, former editor of Psychology Today magazine, says, "Courage is the by-product of a compassionate community," reminding us how critical it is to be vigilant in our choices of traveling companions. You will begin to learn that over-zealous team players, those that rain on your parade or offer uninvited criticism, belong a healthy distance from your prodigy. You will become able to identify toxic people and situations as they arise. You will take responsibility for the ways you use people and circumstances to distract, undermine, and sabotage your best intentions.

The process of cleaning house requires you marginalize the people (even parents when necessary) that are holding you back. These are the people that say they support your dreams, but whenever you're finished spending time with them, you feel drained, depressed, guilty, selfish, or derailed. Cleaning house also includes cleaning yourself out of others' houses that are toxic to you and your dreams. By releasing the dead weight, you release a vast storehouse of energy and generate a tidal wave of momentum.

Prodigy Story:

Denise is an extremely gifted commercial designer. Over the years, however, she bounced around from company to company and never really enjoyed the fruits of her labor or discovered how to take her gift to the level of calling. As I got to know Denise, it became obvious she had never really cleaned house. She worked for employers that usurped her accomplishments; her best friends were self-centered and belittled her successes; and her family stood waiting for her to fall into her addictions or despair after every project. Toxic people plus toxic situations equal a frustrating and painful life to which there seems to be no way out. As Denise began to identify all the places and people in her life that were toxic to her well-being, dreams, and calling, she came to see how she unconsciously fabricated them to fulfill her internalized negative core beliefs. As she recognized that she was the one destroying what she was trying to create—by allowing these people too close to her dream—she became capable of dealing appropriately with each person.

The first person Denise decided to take responsibility for was her best friend. As she looked at the feelings of inadequacy and low self-esteem that she always felt after sharing her accomplishments with her friend, Denise realized that she could no longer answer her friend's inquiries about her work life with details or feelings. The first few times Denise practiced restraint she felt like she was an unloving, selfish friend. She told me that doing this was one of the hardest things she'd ever done. As she began marginalizing or eliminating other friends and associates who weren't really supportive, her feelings of being a horrible person gave way to a new sense of empowerment and self-esteem. These new feelings were accompanied by a level of commitment to herself and her work that inspired her to do the same with the members of her family who demeaned her accomplishments and always projected the worst.

The next place Denise cleaned house was at work. She recognized that being there was not only making her unhappy, it was beginning to make her ill. She felt that her boss was a tyrant and a perfectionist who didn't care about the quality of her employees' lives, only how dedicated they were to her and her business. In a face-to-face discussion with her boss, Denise, terrified and feeling very vulnerable, shared her feelings. She told her boss that though she loved her work and knew it to be her calling, she could no longer work there under the existing conditions. Denise's boss was so moved by her honesty and integrity that she confessed feeling that her own life was out of control and she had not been aware she was taking it out on her employees. She asked Denise to list everything that wasn't working for her. The following Monday, in the weekly staff meeting, Denise's boss shared her list of grievances, invited the other employees to voice their feelings and then instituted most of the changes Denise recommended. A miraculous house cleaning took place as a result of Denise's willingness to parent her prodigy within. Denise is now given the plum design jobs and has brought her passion for ecologically sound design and products to the company. As a result of Denise's courage to clean house, not only have her job, friends, and quality of life improved tremendously, but she's also expanded her calling by becoming an advocate for "green design" in the corporate world.

Prodigy Practice #11 – Toxic People: Identify those who don't support your Prodigy.

• Firing The Committee – Gaining Freedom From the Internalized Cult of "Not Enough"

One of the basic difficulties you will encounter when first attempting to give life to the prodigy within is a tendency to fall prey to the ferocious rant of The Committee. The Committee is not some external group out to get you, but the internalized voices and thought forms that constantly undermine your best intentions. Unseating The Committee is a formidable task; it starts with re-educating yourself from the ground up by examining negative self-talk, unconscious thought forms, "harmless" distractions and sudden urges that dissipate momentum and destroy your Intentions. The Committee can be the internalized voices of an unsupportive parent, a teacher who's "got it in for you," the boss who told you you'd never amount to anything, or your own low self-esteem disguised as consideration. No matter how The Committee manifests, it must be identified, uprooted and reprogrammed.

Being the victim of The Committee is like being a member of a cult. Over the years you stop questioning its authority, turn your will and decisions over to The Committee's agenda and ultimately submit yourself to fulfilling someone else's Intentions. The tyrannical grip of The Committee ends up robbing you of your personal power and freedom to be who you really are. The most effective way to eliminate The Committee's dictatorial influence is to employ the deprogramming techniques used to free cult members from the negative "group-think" that has taken over their minds and lives.

The Three Phases to Deprogram The Committee are:

Phase 1: Identify the Voice of The Committee. In order to identify who is speaking for The Committee you must 1) pay attention to how you talk yourself out of things you think you want; 2) identify the internalized undermining comments, truisms, and criticisms spoken originally by parents, teachers, and authority figures; and 3) examine the experiences you consider failures and determine the negative inner vocalizations and feelings you generated as a result of those experiences.

> *To be independent of public opinion is the first formal condition of achieving anything great.*
>
> G.W.F. Hegel

Phase 2: Uproot The Committee. Once you've begun to recognize the wide variety of voices employed by The Committee, uprooting requires you to 1) identify which situations result in The Committee taking over. In other words, does it happen when you are overwhelmed, unprepared, at the peak of your power, in the presence of someone you envy, or when you are poised for success? 2) determine what tactics it employs and how you respond to them. Does it distract, depress, deflate, despoil, or delude you? 3) be aware of how you give away your personal power and freedom to The Committee. Do you run and hide, find a way to prove it correct by doing exactly what it says, rebel by doing the exact opposite, or do you simply believe that The Committee speaks the truth and fighting it is hopeless?

Phase 3: Reprogram The Committee. Reprogramming requires vigilance and the marginalization of anyone who works or speaks for The Committee. This requires that you 1) pay attention to every time The Committee attempts to assert its position. At times the voice will come from within you (remember it's not you); sometimes it's from someone else. Either way you must be vigilant, countering The Committee's words with awareness, affirmations, and a positive direction; 2) replace the negative rant of The Committee with clarity and insight by using your Prodigy Support System (Prodigy Champions, mentors, and peers); 3) have a full arsenal of homeopathic remedies, comebacks, retorts, and affirmations at your disposal whenever and wherever The Committee rears its ugly head.

Prodigy Story:

When Elaine was a little girl she told her mother she wanted to be a teacher. Her mother told her, "You can't be a teacher. You'll never make enough money; you're really not good at those kinds of things and besides, you have epilepsy. Imagine if you had a seizure in front of those poor children. Honey, you should be a dental hygienist. They make good money and it offers a lot of security." In one fell swoop her mother armed The Committee with a lifetime's worth of rational responses to any situation. Elaine internalized her mother's words as The Committee's rant. She went on to become a dental hygienist, letting go of her dream and any sense of her calling along the way.

Though Elaine grew to enjoy her work as a dental hygienist and received a degree of personal satisfaction from it, she was happy to let it go when she got married and began raising a family. When her husband found himself without a job, however, she went back to work to pick up the slack. For the next nine years, Elaine went about earning a living without giving it much thought until one day she had a vision. It recurred daily for the next nine months. In this vision Elaine saw her tombstone, which read, "Elaine Sherman Glazer, Dental Hygienist." It haunted and terrified her. "I realized that I was going to live and die and never explore what I felt was my calling. I was never going to know what more I could have given in this life." She knew she couldn't continue on the same blind path, but she didn't know what to do. Then one day, as she was preparing to clean a patient's teeth, she couldn't manage to close her hand around the dental tool. For what seemed like an eternity she struggled to pick the tool up, to no avail. She knew, between the recurring vision and this episode, that the time had come to re-examine where her life was headed. She made a promise to herself to get applications from four universities and find a way to become a social worker.

> *The wise man knows that he has only one enemy – himself. This is an enemy difficult to ignore and full of cunning. It assails one with doubts and fears.*
>
> Ben Hecht

Her friends and family questioned the sanity of her decision but the greatest resistance came from within; The Committee, speaking in her mother's voice said, "You're 46 years old. In five more years you'll get your pension; you'd be stupid to lose that. Besides, you'll be competing with people half your age, and you'll never be accepted anyway." Elaine was accepted to four prestigious universities but still that did not quell The Committee. Even with the support of family and friends the rant continued. Knowing this was something she had to do, she joined a support group and began the long and painful process of Firing the Committee.

A month before graduating Elaine searched the classified ads to see what jobs might be available. She saw an ad from the Epilepsy Foundation for a social worker and, on a fluke, went in for an interview. "I didn't think I stood a chance, there were hundreds of people more qualified than I was and I wasn't even out of school yet," she says. (Obviously The Committee was in session.) Elaine was stunned when she was offered the position and was asked to start immediately.

When Elaine graduated she was not only the oldest student, but also the only one with a full-time job. That day, for the first time in her life, Elaine knew her mother had been wrong. She felt free from the limitations she had internalized as her own truth for the previous forty years. She had done a first-rate job of Firing the Committee and, in the process, discovered her calling.

In Elaine's new position she enjoyed the extraordinary satisfaction of counseling others who suffered, as she had, from the effects of epilepsy. As a result of her success as a therapist, she realized her childhood dream of teaching by training others how to support and care for those with epilepsy. In our last conversation Elaine told me: "It's not easy to Fire the Committee. Though you never get rid of it altogether, you do get to the point where it no longer keeps you from doing the right thing. For that I am very grateful."

Prodigy Practice #12 – Deprogram: Eliminate the Negative Influence of the Committee.

- The Power of Unreasonable Expectations

President John F. Kennedy created what many believed to be an entirely Unreasonable Expectation when he set the goal to "land a man on the moon and return him home safely before the end of the decade." His Unreasonable Expectation mobilized thousands of people, ignited the dreams of a nation, and created a collective expectation that made it so. We know Thomas Edison, Susan B. Anthony, Tiger Woods, Madame Curie, and Mahatma Gandhi as a result of the Unreasonable Expectations each of them held. Each believed, without knowing how it would come to pass, that their Expectations were entirely reasonable and that it was actually their detractors whose thinking was small, ill-conceived, and rooted in the past.

In the long run you hit only what you aim at. Therefore, though you should fail immediately, you had better aim at something high.

Thoreau

Unreasonable Expectations often start with only you believing in them. As you attract others to believe, you gain momentum and begin to transform your expectation into faith. Eventually the "collective wisdom" regarding the unlikelihood of attaining your Unreasonable Expectation changes. Your hitherto impossible vision is embraced and the assumption that it was always going to happen prevails. The electric light, women's right to vote, the discovery of uranium, and India's independence all attest to the "collective wisdom" being shattered by the power of an Unreasonable Expectation.

The journey from believing that an expectation is unreasonable to expecting the best concludes when you successfully 1) disavow the undermining beliefs perpetuated by The Committee; 2) trust the power of your Intention and the ingenuity of the prodigy within to conjure an otherwise unpredictable solution; and 3) recognize the way your true expectations have always manifested. This last one may prove to be the most challenging. The idea that you always manifest your expectations, consciously or unconsciously, may be a hard pill to swallow, but just considering the possibility is an excellent way to begin to take responsibility for how you have supported and undermined your prodigy's will. It's as easy as asking yourself, "How did I participate in this outcome?" As you recognize how you've manifested your expectations, you will see your thoughts, words, and unspoken expectations for what they really are: supportive or undermining.

Prodigy Story:

One of the most inspiring stories of the power of an Unreasonable Expectation was Mahatma Gandhi's expectation to liberate his country from the tyranny of foreign rule through non-violence. At first no one took him seriously—not his fellow countrymen and certainly not the British. It was obvious from the newspaper cartoon drawings around the world, depicting a lone man in a loincloth defeating the British Fleet with a spinning wheel that no one took him very seriously. But they did not know the power of Unreasonable Expectations in the hands and heart of a man with a clearly articulated calling.

We all know the story of what happened. Slowly, Gandhi's Unreasonable Expectation grew among the Untouchables, the lowest level of people in the Indian caste system. It then found its way into the hearts and minds of all of the Indian people. Still unaware of the power of what Gandhi had set into motion, the British thought they could quell the movement toward independence the way they had in every other country they had occupied: by violence. That would prove to be their biggest mistake. They were so busy laughing at the "Naked Indian" that they were totally unaware that his expectation of a non-violent revolution had grown into "an idea whose time has come" among a critical mass of Indians. When thousands of unarmed Indians peacefully stood their ground and were injured or killed by British soldiers, the snowball turned into an avalanche. From that point on, the world took the little man's dream quite seriously, and it was just a matter of time before his Unreasonable Expectation finally became Britain's reality as well.

Prodigy Practice #13 – Five Achievable, Unreasonable Expectations

• Positive Knowing – Developing a Positive and Irrefutable Belief in Your Calling

Most prodigies I've researched, from Beethoven to Picasso, believed that they had a unique gift and a definite calling. Though they might have been hypercritical of something they did or created, they rarely doubted that they were "one of a kind" and destined for great things. Even when they lost their bearings, they rarely lost their belief in their uniqueness and their calling. When Muhammad Ali said, "I am the greatest!" he wasn't simply manipulating his opponent, he was speaking his truth. Tiger Woods acknowledges that much of his success is the result of his parents' unconditional belief in him, the subliminal tapes he listened to daily, and the positive knowing that called him to demolish every one of his hero's, Jack Nicklaus, records. Do you think anyone would ever attempt to climb Mt. Everest unless they were absolutely convinced they would be successful?

Prodigies employ every possible means to sustain and enhance their positive knowing. In order to fortify themselves for the challenges ahead, they will try every trick in the book: affirmations, the undying belief of a loved one, science, their own uncommon sense, or devaluing the existing "agreement realities" about what is possible. Jim Ryan knew, based on uncommon sense, that the existing belief that the human body would never break the four-minute mile barrier was just that: a belief. He knew he was destined to prove all of the naysayers wrong. Many of the greatest accomplishments have resulted from a positive knowing that accelerated the "knowers" toward their goal.

Though it's essential to surround yourself with people who believe in you, it isn't until you believe in yourself and your intrinsic calling that you can focus on manifesting your prodigy's plan for you. Though you may still not know the exact nature of your calling, developing a clear and precise Purpose Statement will enhance your confidence and serve as a lodestar for navigating you toward it. Now that you've clarified your gifts, passions, pastimes, strengths, weaknesses, and undermining tendencies; you have generated the kind of self-knowledge necessary to formulate your Purpose Statement.

I had a sense of destiny as though my life was assigned to me by fate and had to be fulfilled. This gave me an inner security . . . . Often I had the feeling that in all decisive matters, I was no longer among men, but was alone with God.

"Memories, Dreams, Reflections"

The first time I considered my possible Purpose Statement, I stumbled upon a memory that perfectly embodied my prodigy. From ages eight to ten I would steal cigarettes and matches from my mother and go into the gardeners' shed behind our house. I'd crack the door just enough to let a narrow plane of sunlight through. With barely containable excitement, I'd light the cigarette (I wasn't interested in the cigarette, only the smoke), put my face into the sunlight and blow a gentle steady stream of smoke into the light. Transfixed, in an ecstatic state, I sat spellbound as the silver-blue smoke swirled and glowed hypnotically. I couldn't steal enough cigarettes to satisfy my curiosity. The power of reliving this memory reminded me that, over and over again, in one way or another, throughout my life, I've attempted to recreate this experience, this state of mind, for others and myself. As I allowed the feelings of this experience to fill me with the same ecstatic feelings of that time, my prodigy's Purpose Statement exploded in my awareness: "I create immersive, transformative, spiritually uplifting experiences." Whether making a 3-D IMAX movie, designing a retail store, teaching yoga, branding a company, or writing this book, it has always been the same: My prodigy is fully alive, I am fully alive, when I'm creating immersive, transformative, spiritually uplifting experiences.

Prodigy Story:

Nathan produced one of the highest grossing children's movies of all time, earning over $400 million worldwide. Prior to this he successfully produced two other critically and financially successful movies featuring some of the biggest movie stars of our era. Nathan loved making movies, believed it was his calling, and was prepared to do it for the rest of his life, but the universe had other plans for him. In spite of the box office success of his children's movie, the sequel was ripped out of his hands by the movie studio and turned over to someone else to produce. Following several unsuccessful attempts to launch other feature films Nathan began to feel that he'd lost his "mojo" in the film business. Having burned through his producing fee living the "lifestyle," Nathan found himself nearly broke, out of work, and a pariah in an industry that depends on connections. With his tail between his legs, Nathan got his real estate license.

Within a couple of months, it was obvious real estate did not fit his personality or his Archetypes of Service.

Angry, frustrated, and beyond confused, Nathan was driven to ask the question; "What do you want for me?" His wife, knowing that one of his good friends had fled the movie business and landed on his feet as a high school teacher, suggested that Nathan take a job as a substitute teacher until he figured out what to do. The next film job never came, but in the meantime Nathan was hired as a long-term substitute at an excellent junior high school. At the end of the year, the tides miraculously turned and Nathan had a full-time job, even though he didn't have his teaching credential yet. Though he had never planned to be a teacher and considered it an enormous fall from grace, he felt it was God-given and he was not about to throw it away.

When Nathan and I first spoke he told me that after two years he was just beginning to get a handle on the teaching thing and still wasn't sure what role it was going to play in the overall scope of his life. Though he was enjoying the challenge, he wasn't sure if it was really his calling. I suggested that, whether it was or wasn't his life's purpose, maybe he could find a way to align it with his calling. When I asked Nathan to describe the underlying themes of the films he'd produced, it didn't take more than a couple of seconds for him to confidently exclaim, "I love taking ordinary people and unlocking the extraordinary within them," to which I replied, "Sounds like the kind of guy I'd want as my teacher." I suggested that he align his teaching with what he loved to do and make every book assignment, every essay, and every lecture an extension of his incredibly clear and potent Purpose Statement. By simply doing this, he would not only be acting in harmony with his life's purpose but also fulfilling it.

As a result of Nathan clarifying his Purpose Statement, his previously fuzzy perspective on teaching came into sharp, clear focus. Relieved of wondering whether or not he's fulfilling his "life's purpose," Nathan now focuses his energy on doing what he feels he was put here to do and lets the universe guide him to greater opportunities to give the gift he loves to give.

Prodigy Practice #14 – Strengths as Calling: Enhance your confidence by building your sense of knowingness.

CHAPTER 5

Principle #3: PRACTICE MAKES PRODIGY

Whether you're an athlete, artist, scientist or entrepreneur, there is nothing as personally rewarding or as likely to generate success as daily practice and an active, unfailing commitment to show up for your calling. Eddie Van Halen, widely considered one of the greatest guitarists of all time, took his guitar everywhere as a teenager. He practiced all the time, wherever he was. He was not a born prodigy; he was a prodigy with regard to his commitment to his passion for playing guitar. More than any other element it is this kind of commitment that distinguishes prodigies. It's been my experience that the kind of commitment exhibited by prodigies from Van Halen to Einstein to Michael Jordan is far easier to generate when you are pursuing that singular thing that is yours alone to do, that you love doing. In short, practice makes prodigy. Michelangelo put it all in perspective when he said, "If people knew how hard I worked to get my mastery, it wouldn't seem so wonderful after all." The key to practicing daily is passion, love, and joy for the activity, not the outcome itself.

- Every Day in Every Way

Prodigies are both born and created. The misguided belief that anyone could write a symphony like Mozart or paint like Michelangelo just because they're born with a great gift is a myth that has persisted for centuries. Every child prodigy's extraordinary success is the result of hard work and perseverance. Mozart, under the stern and demanding tutelage of his father (who was considered the best music teacher in Austria), worked every day in every way to develop his innate talent.

> *It is well with me only when I have a chisel in my hand.*
>
> Michelangelo

Though every one of us is born with our own unique gifts, few rise to the heights of a Michael Jordan, Magic Johnson or Lance Armstrong. Yes, they were all born with good bones, musculature, size and dexterity, but it's common knowledge that among their peers, no one practiced harder, more consistently or with more dedication. In fact, there's nothing prodigies would rather do, every day in every way, than what they love.

When you consider your dreams and goals you must consider what it's going to take to achieve them: a consistent, focused, unwavering regimen of practice, education and readjustment. No one can tell you exactly what that's going to look like. Only you know.

What matters is that you discover what you need to do, make time to nourish the prodigy within and use your available resources and opportunities wisely. A full time job, children or untold responsibilities cannot be used as an excuse if you intend to embody the prodigy within. You do not need to practice 12 hours a day; you need to shift your priorities to free up as much time and energy as you can. Though a 12-hour-per-day time commitment might be necessary to play first violin with the New York Philharmonic, it is not critical to realizing your dream in the initial phase of unfolding your calling. As you generate a clear Intention to fulfill your calling, practice regularly, and cultivate your skills; the universe will open up an abundance of space and time for you to shift your energies to your dream. Having made the decision, you need only show up with consistency, passion, and impeccability, every day in every way, and all the opportunities you need to express your calling will be revealed to you.

> *Any devout man can do as much as I have done, if he worked as hard.*
>
> Johann Sebastian Bach

Prodigy Story:

Consider the high school boy of diminutive stature, who (at 5'6" tall) was obsessed with playing pro basketball. He practiced twice as hard as his teammates, learned every trick he could, perpetually pestered his heroes, memorized all the plays, and practiced dunking over a thousand times before his first successful dunk. When he tried out for his school team he was dismissed as too short and placed on the junior varsity team. It was only through his extraordinary dedication to hard work and the sheer tenacity of his will that he eventually convinced the coach to let him play on the Varsity team. As a Varsity player he went on to score over 25 points a game, lead his team to the playoffs and be voted Player of the Year. Reminded every day, in almost every way, that he'd never make it to the pros due to his "shortcomings," Spud Webb never gave up on dream. Instead, at 22 years of age Spud Webb became the smallest starting player on a pro basketball team and the shortest man to ever win the prestigious Slam Dunk Contest. Spud is proof positive of what Edison had to say about his own successes: "One percent inspiration and ninety-nine percent perspiration."

Prodigy Practice #15 – Prodigy Time: Create a realistic schedule for unfolding your Calling.

- Fail Often, Fail Fast

Though they don't appear to fail, most prodigies attribute their success to their willingness to take big risks, fall short of their goals, and pick themselves up and try again. They have an immense appetite for studying and learning from their mistakes. Michael Jordan claims the reason he was so successful was he failed more often than anyone he knew. As a young boy, when Tiger Woods lost a match, he and his father would spend hours to determine why he lost, create a program to address his shortcomings, and would often work on them that very day.

> *Fail Better.*
>
> Samuel Beckett

Prodigies must determine their own definition of failure, learn to course-correct and, without exception, recommit to trying again and again. No one successfully liberates the prodigy within who doesn't understand every success is preceded by innumerable failures. Know that failing is an essential milestone on the road to success for every prodigy.

To reach the pinnacle of your potential, you must learn to recognize your Failure Response Strategy (FRS). Do you avoid work, sink into the TV, pig out on ice cream or anesthetize yourself with alcohol, drugs or chaos? Do you do all or several of the above? Once you've identified your FRS you're free to devise appropriate remedies to avoid the potential stagnation and self-destruction that most often accompanies these undermining tendencies. As you become adept at identifying your Failure Response Strategies and act appropriately, you actually gain momentum, thus accelerating through what used to grind you to a stop and result in failure.

> *Reward excellent failures.*
>
> *Punish mediocre success.*
>
> Tom Peters

Prodigy Story:

One of my favorite examples of "fail often, fail fast" is based on Thomas Edison's quest to invent the electric light. Edison had no doubt in his mind that it was his calling to invent the electric light and light up the world. At the point in his career that he committed to inventing the light bulb he had the world's largest laboratory, JP Morgan's wealth behind him, and no doubt in his mind that he was the man and this was the time. After many, many months and hundreds of failed experiments Edison finally succeeded. In the interviews that followed Edison's discovery he was asked if he ever believed he was wasting his time or chasing a chimera; his reply reveals the source of his success: "The electric light has caused me the greatest amount of study and has required the most elaborate experiments. I have constructed 3,000 different theories in connection with the electric light, each of them reasonable and apparently likely to be true. Yet in two cases only did my experiments prove the truth of my theory." When pressed he went on to say, "I was never inclined to be hopeless of success. I cannot say the same for all of my associates … the trouble with other inventors is they try a few things and quit. I never quit until I get what I want."

Edison knew his strengths. He knew his purpose. He knew what he was Called to do. He knew everything in his life had led him to this moment and the brink of success. He knew every experiment he had ever undertaken required hundreds of failed attempts and dozens of wrong turns. He knew it was these "failures" that not only showed him what didn't work, but also defined which direction to turn next. The positive knowing that Edison expressed, over and over again, allowed him to weather failures without giving up or turning back. What was often referred to as arrogance, stubbornness, and misguided efforts by his competitors, was in fact nothing more than the wisdom that comes from knowing every success is preceded by a truckload of failure. Edison knew the surest and fastest way to success was to fail often and fail fast.

Prodigy Practice #16 – Failure Response Strategy: How do you respond to Failure?

- A Tolerance For Ambiguity

While most of us need only hear a confusing or discouraging word to be thrown into a nosedive, prodigies not only tolerate confusion and ambiguity but also are most often fueled by it. If things don't go as planned, they find a way to adapt. They've learned, through repeated experience, the biggest breakthroughs most often occur after prolonged periods of ambiguity, confusion, and having exhausted every conceivable possibility. It is this inherent understanding of the critical role that chaos plays in discovery, creativity, and development that inspires successful prodigies to remain active, directed, and alert. They have learned that gaining a tolerance for ambiguity generates the perfect atmosphere for breakthroughs to occur and for new directions mysteriously to appear.

> *The belief that anything is possible seems to be the most efficient belief working in my life. There is always a solution within the specific situation that may not be obvious on the surface.*
>
> Carol Adrienne
>
> *The Purpose of Your Life*

A tolerance for ambiguity is nothing more than the willingness to remain alert when there's nothing to focus on, to persevere when you have no idea where you're going or what you are doing, and to become an explorer when you've strayed into a foreign land. When you feel trapped in a dense tangle of vines, you've got to be willing to sit down and await inspiration, climb a tree for perspective or backtrack until the sun burns through the mist. Prodigies have learned, all too painfully, the best way to move forward at these times is to move sideways, backwards or elsewhere. Rudyard Kipling said, "I have learned that when the inner helper is in charge, do not try to think consciously. Drift … wait … and obey." Every prodigy must discover his or her own way to deal with chaos and ambiguity, whether it's taking a walk in nature, talking to a mentor or leaping wholeheartedly into a night of inspired debauchery.

Prodigy Story:

I had been working for many years as a concept designer when jobs suddenly dried up. I had been at the top of my field and the top of my game when, inexplicably, I was out of work and out of luck. I tried everything to jump-start my career. I shifted from retail design back to museum design and then from film to television but the universe had decided it was time for me to move on. I was not only confused but, to add insult to injury, the only work I could find was as a handyman. I remember wondering, "What went wrong? What did I do to deserve this? Why have I fallen from grace?" I was drowning in chaos and ambiguity.

While I was working as a not-so-humble carpenter, a friend who I'd not seen in seven years called with an offer I couldn't refuse. My friend, a registered nurse and cranio-sacral therapist, told me a group that was planning to franchise holistic health centers had just recruited her. She had suggested they hire me to help them define their direction, generate a viable plan of action, and organize their corporate structure. I must admit it was so contrary to the life I was living at the time that I felt a bit like a fraud when they flew me first-class to Kentucky to spearhead their effort. Talk about ambiguity — one day I was spackling ceilings for 20 bucks an hour, the next day I was earning $800 a day designing the future of a multi-million dollar start-up. Had I stopped for a moment to consider my limited knowledge of the field, my lack of business acumen, or the sheer weight and scope of the project; I would have folded up shop immediately. But I didn't. Instead, my tolerance for ambiguity allowed me to perceive the entire undertaking as an extension of what I'd been doing for the previous fifteen years, conceptually designing enormous projects. Once the initial phase of design was over, I was hired to coach and consult the principles of the four companies that comprised the core of the franchise. Without any clue that my life might take such an unexpected left turn, I was suddenly in a new and challenging field, applying previously developed skills in completely different ways, and being valued for bringing "fresh, original ideas and the kind of people skills needed for the centers to be successful."

The job carved a path to a new life. Over the next couple of years similar opportunities arrived at my door, all unannounced. The work was challenging and a source of tremendous joy, and now, in retrospect, I see it as the hand of benevolent intent guiding me toward writing this book. The things I learned consulting for companies, coaching individuals, and creating strategies to maximize the employees' gifts has been inspirational and pivotal to all that I've embraced as my calling — to create opportunities for others to re-connect with their prodigy within, share their gift, and discover their calling.

> *When I work, I relax. Doing nothing ... makes me tired.*
>
> Picasso

Prodigy Practice #17 – Changing Gears: When you hit the wall, how do you adapt?

- Every Moment Counts

Prodigies use every spare moment, live frugally when necessary, and fight for the space and time to do their thing. When you understand that doing anything to develop your gift is an investment in your future, then reading about Van Gogh while on the treadmill, writing during your lunch hour or practicing on an imaginary keyboard in solitary confinement are all powerful ways to support the prodigy within. One of the keys to making every moment count is skewing all of your activities—work, entertainment, reading and relationships—toward enhancing your gift. When you've generated enough of these small and seemingly insignificant efforts you are not only nourishing the prodigy within but also setting the stage for opportunity to knock.

Though all of us need to earn a living, demanding the emerging prodigy to generate your primary source of income prematurely is like sending your ten-year-old out to support the family. No matter what you need to do to support yourself or your family, you must allow the prodigy within to find its way to financial freedom at its own speed. In the meantime, it's up to you to guard your free time and the sanctity of the prodigy with the ferocity of a mother lion.

Prodigy Story:

When you think you just can't find the time, energy or money to work toward your dream, consider my friend Patty, who, with two small children, paints for an hour at five o'clock in the morning before they wake up, another hour during their midday nap, and two to three more hours after they've gone to sleep at night. With her dedication knowing no bounds, Patty figured out how to save an additional $50 per week out of her food allowance to hire someone to take the children out for three hours, twice a week. After a year-and-a-half of working passionately on her art, making every moment count, Patty accumulated a large body of original work, had her first one-woman show, garnered rave reviews in the local paper, enjoyed several sales, and received a number of commissions. One of Patty's biggest successes grew out of donating a painting to a large national charity to be auctioned at their annual fundraiser. She was astounded when the bidding reached twice the price she believed her painting was worth and prompted several other sales, all for even more money. The success that resulted from making every moment count has afforded Patty the freedom to quit her part-time job, hire a nanny to help with the housework and the children, and paint full-time.

Prodigy Practice #18 – Time Wasters: What do you do to squander and waste time?

Chapter 6

Principle #4:
SEEK UPLIFTING SOURCES OF INSPIRATION

When Mozart stated, "There is not a great master whose works I have not frequently and diligently studied," he revealed his debt to those who had preceded and inspired him. Prodigies seek inspiration from any and every source available. They often choose to work and play with those who have far more knowledge, skill and experience than they have. They use what they've learned from every person who has preceded them. They embrace their heroes' strengths, learn from their weaknesses and emulate elements of their style. Prodigies seek uplifting sources of inspiration by cultivating mentors, listening to their muse and embracing motivation wherever they find it.

When I first set off to learn to paint, I read the biographies of all of my favorite artists. Prior to reading these biographies, I was of the opinion that great artists were born with their gift wholly intact. To my surprise, every artist I studied spent a prolonged period of time perfecting their craft by making exact copies of other artists' masterpieces. All great prodigies understand the words of Captain Ahab when speaking of his mentor, Moby Dick: "I love all men who dive. Any fish can swim near the surface, but it takes a great whale to go downstairs five miles or more." If you want to go as high and deep and far as you possibly can, it is a good idea to seek those who have successfully plumbed their own heights and depths. A true mentor is a guide, a promise, a traveling companion and a constant inspiration.

- A Steady Diet of Inspiration – An Infusion of Inspiration

Your prodigy requires a steady diet of inspiration. Just like a small child, the prodigy is extremely curious, drawn to explore and interact with anything that captures its interest and jump-starts the imagination. By cultivating and indulging your interest in everything that lights your fuse, you 1) rehabilitate your natural curiosity; 2) refine your intuition (establishing a clear channel of communication with your prodigy); and 3) feed your spirit a steady diet of inspiration.

In the initial phase of reconnecting with the prodigy it is essential to "follow your bliss" and cultivate a voracious appetite for things that turn you on. Art, nature, juggling, puzzles, bird watching, video games, unexplored worlds—anything and everything can be grist for the inspiration mill. When you give yourself permission to scratch an inexplicable itch, to play without consideration of outcome, and to create in whatever way you want, you transform the dirt road to oblivion into a super-highway to your calling. Whenever

I question people who are actively and joyously engaged in their life's work, they always refer to how inspired they are every day they get to live and give their gift. In my experience, those who have found ways to feed their prodigy a steady diet of inspiration rapidly find their way to their calling.

Prodigy Story:

"Did you ever see the rain with Georgia? Did you ever watch a great storm? There was never anyone in the world like her in her appreciation of such things." These are the words of one of Georgia O'Keeffe's students from her early days of teaching high school in Texas. Throughout her life, Georgia O'Keeffe sought inspiration from every conceivable source. She had art teachers throughout her childhood and into her twenties. She often acknowledged how each of her teachers inspired in her the desire to continuously experiment as a painter. She loved to garden. She played the piano and violin. She was an avid reader of adventures, travel books, history and the plays of Euripides and Chekov. She read and re-read Kandinsky's *Art of Spiritual Harmony*, each time inspired to rethink art. She studied the art of Van Gogh, Rodin, Picasso, and the Orientalists. As a grown woman, she spoke of a pen and ink drawing she saw when she was 13 years old that so inspired her she said, "That picture started something in me that has had to do with the everlasting urge that makes me keep on painting."

Ultimately, the greatest source of inspiration in Georgia's life came from nature. As a child in the Dakotas, she walked to school in every kind of weather, taking her inspiration from the fields of grain, great oak trees, rough-tongued cows, and clammy-skinned frogs. As she grew up, she came to depend on the beauty and solitude of nature for inspiration: canyons, sunsets, lakes, flowers, lightning, the open desert sky, the now famous whitewashed cow skulls—all food for the soul. Her skill and impact as an artist continued to grow throughout her life as she continued to supply herself with a steady diet of inspiration. Georgia O'Keeffe's commitment to find inspiration in every aspect of her life has earned her the reputation as one of the most inspired and inspiring artists of the twentieth century.

Prodigy Practice #19 – Prodigy Date: People, places, and activities that inspire you.

- Heroes, Mentors, and Peak Performers

The Hindus believe that the greatest gift one can give a teacher is to surpass the teacher's accomplishments. Bach was set on tumbling Handel as the greatest composer, Michael Jordan planned on out-scoring Dr. J, and Tiger Woods fixated on demolishing every one of Jack Nicklaus' records. There is a time in all prodigies' careers when they mimic their heroes or predecessors, learning from their triumphs and failures. By doing this they gain perspective, turn the greats into mentors, and mingle with their "peers." A day comes when, having learned everything they can from their heroes, prodigies resolve to surpass or shatter their heroes accomplishments. Leonardo da Vinci spent years painting in the exact style of his mentor. When he began to receive his own commissions da Vinci left his mentor and his style with the resolution to surpass all his mentor's accomplishments.

Every peak performer I've studied and interviewed values and acknowledges the gifts their mentors have given them. Every one of them believes, without the help of their mentors, they would never have achieved the level of success they had dreamt about. Think about it, if you wanted to go to the Olympics, would you try to get there without researching and analyzing those who had already achieved success in your field? Would you try to do it without the help of a mentor or a coach? Preparing to live a life inspired by the prodigy within is just as challenging and just as elusive. Heroes, mentors, and peak performers are the companions, guides and teachers that help you successfully navigate the tumultuous currents leading to the fulfillment of your calling.

> *The mentor, as opposed to the guru, is the one who is there to help you make up your own mind, light your own fire, unfold your own myth. True mentorship draws out your mind, draws out your hidden qualities, puts the bellows to the soul, fans the flame, develops the gold that the mentor is trying to draw out. The mentor is the power of wisdom outside of the family because parents in this kind of mythological speaking cannot be mentors.*
>
> *"Once and Future Myths"*
>
> Phil Cousineau

It's my experience that at every point in our lives there's at least one person that qualifies as a mentor. Whether formal or informal, if someone (or their books, music or paintings) has been an inspiration, a personal guide, or just a sounding board, they probably qualify as a mentor. Sometimes mentors have nothing to do with the arena of your calling, but the mastery they exhibit in their life inspires you to deepen your relationship with your prodigy within. You may have heroes you've never met whose careers you have followed religiously. By continually referring to their accomplishments, actions, and humanity for guidance, you turn an otherwise unreachable hero into a powerful personal mentor.

Prodigy Stories:

The film Searching for Bobby Fisher presents the best example of almost every principle in this book. Josh, in the true spirit of child prodigies, learns to play chess simply by watching the speed players in New York City's Washington Park. The parents of eight-year-old Josh are both mentors and heroes; they support him and his gift in every conceivable way. The mother is protective but encouraging, allowing him to play with the street-savvy, cigarette-smoking, fringy speed chess players in Washington Park. In unabashed support of her fledgling prodigy, Josh's mother shells out five dollars for him to play—and beat—a former Grandmaster. His father hires a "practice, practice, practice, study, study, study," style disciplinarian to polish his son's skills and sees to it that the disciplinarian is balanced by a speed player whose passion and love of the game inspires his son. At one point Josh's father defends him before a concerned teacher who questions how this "chess thing" is affecting Josh's schoolwork. In a scene I still can't watch without crying (and wishing I had a father who believed in me like that) Josh's father rebukes the teacher by saying, "You want to know how good he is at this (chess)? He is better at this than I have ever been at anything in my life. He is better at this than you (the teacher) will ever be at anything. My son has a gift... and once you acknowledge that then maybe we'll have something to talk about."

As Josh ascends through the chess ranks, his father/mentor helps him remain balanced by playing ball with him and taking him fly-fishing for two weeks, no chess allowed. Each of the characters represents the variety of forms heroes, mentors and peak performers take in the life of the prodigy as it unfolds, develops, and obtains mastery.

Prior to the final chess match in the movie, Josh receives the long-withheld acknowledgment of the disciplinarian mentor in the form of a beautifully framed certificate inscribed, "This is to certify that Josh Waitzkin, on this day, has, in the eyes of his teacher, attained the rank of Grandmaster." His mentor, choking with emotion, goes on to say, "I have never been so proud of anyone in my life. I am honored to call myself your teacher." Following this, Josh wins the state championships, where he graciously acknowledges each of his mentors for the gifts they have given him. And then, in the final scene of the movie, nine-year-old Josh, walking with his arm around the shoulder of a less gifted seven-year-old player who has just been berated by his father, assumes the role of mentor himself when he lovingly states, "Morgan … you want to know a secret? You're a much stronger player than I was at your age."

> *A strong partner guides you through challenges and into excellence … the sheer knowledge that you will be playing with the best lifts you to new heights.*
>
> *"Building Your Field of Dreams"*

Prodigy Practice #20 – Hero Worship: List your heroes, mentors and peak performers.

• Play Up! – Rising to the Challenge

Whether it's competition or apprenticeship, nothing accelerates your abilities and sharpens your skills like playing up—challenging yourself to play or collaborate with someone whose skill level far exceeds your own. In the early days of jazz, every up-and- coming horn player would beg, borrow or steal to jam with Louis Armstrong. As a child, Magic Johnson played basketball with his father and the grown-ups. At ten, Mozart was pitted against the greatest composers of his time. A prodigy will journey a thousand miles to play against the greatest backhand, to spar with the champ, or volunteer to dig with the world's foremost archaeologist. When prodigies stop playing up, it better be because they've become Mecca to their peers.

There have been many times in my life that I've experienced the extraordinary sense of exhilaration that comes from playing up. I have collaborated with the "world's greatest" museum designer, talked philosophy with a Nobel laureate physicist and wrote a script with the national playwright of Korea. I've benefited enormously from playing up; though it can be intimidating, scary and humbling, the payoff has always outweighed the emotional considerations.

Souls are like athletes, that need opponents worthy of them if they are to be tried and extended and pushed to the full use of their powers, and rewarded according to their capacity.

Thomas Merton

Prodigy Story:

When Jack Nicklaus was a young, up-and-coming player, he was offered the opportunity to play up with one of the greatest golfers of all time. The year was 1956 and 16-year-old Jack was playing in his first tournament, the Ohio Open, which was mainly for professionals. During the tournament, he received an unexpected invitation to play an exhibition game with the great Sam Snead. The exhibition game overlapped with the final day of the tournament, so it was arranged that Jack would play his round early at the tournament then fly several hundred miles to the exhibition game. When young Jack arrived at the exhibition game, he had a terrible case of first-tee jitters, but, with no way to escape, he stepped up to play up with the best of the best. In spite of his nervousness, Jack eagerly studied the graceful, flowing swing of the master. Nicklaus later stated that, during the course of the exhibition game, he felt his own "aggressive lash at the ball … magically transformed into a carbon copy of history's all-time smoothest and most graceful golf swing."

Back at the Ohio Open the next morning, Nicklaus shot a 64 and won the championship. Musing many years later, he acknowledged the power of playing up with the Slammer, saying, "Enough of Sam's rhythm rubbed off to make me—at least temporarily—a better player." In true prodigy fashion, Nicklaus had no doubt whom to thank for his inspiration.

Prodigy Practice #21 – Going Up: Create a list of people you can play up with.

- Higher Education – Discover Inventive Modes and Ridiculous Forms of Education.

Though there are legitimate and prescribed routes for gaining knowledge and experience, there comes a time in the life of prodigies when they need to reinvent the wheel to continue developing their gifts. An experienced coach or mentor, seeking to transform their charge's weakest attributes into an unqualified strength, will oftentimes make radical suggestions or devise hair-brained schemes. In the movie Rocky, there's a scene in which Rocky's coach sends him into a freezing cold meat locker to beat the pulp out of hanging sides of beef. The coach knows the primitive act of pulverizing flesh with his bare hands will do Rocky far more good than politely punching a lifeless leather bag. Another memorable movie example takes place in The Karate Kid when Mister Miagi, the mentor, seeking to teach the kid, Daniel, the mindset of karate, has him endlessly waxing the car: "Wax on! Wax off." The Karate Kid perceives having to wax the car as punishment while his mentor knows he's developing the boy's focus, training his muscle memory and teaching him perseverance—all skills necessary to enhance his natural talents.

The higher education of a prodigy often includes developing skills that, though they are not normally associated with your area of expertise, extend and expand your skill, knowledge and talent. Take for example the linebacker who seeks a yoga master to improve his flexibility; the dentist who takes classes from a sculptor to design better crowns; or the golfer who takes private lessons from a grand master in chess to learn strategy. Mastery is twofold: first, it is a measure of one's skill level compared to others in a particular field; second, it is the quality, focus, wisdom, and individuality one brings to the way he or she approaches the work. In the Orient, it is understood that studying with a master, even when the mastery is in a different field, is essential to attaining mastery in one's own field.

Prodigy Story:

For as long as he can remember, Peter has been passionate about traveling to exotic and primitive countries; learning about their cultures, history, and spirituality; and trying to understand the common threads that tie all the cultures of the world together. In his twenties, he dropped out of college because, as he recalls, "I was not learning what I wanted to know, what I felt was really important." Fleeing the upper class British "ghetto" he was raised in, Peter spent the next five years traveling third-class around the world. In the course of his travels, he gained a deep knowledge of many of the arts, the various spiritual traditions, and the unique practices of the indigenous cultures of each of the countries he visited. He also became a collector and authority on the rare cultural artifacts of their various tribes, sects, and societies. In the late sixties, when Peter returned to Britain, his passion had become a full-blown obsession. For six months, he was possessed with sorting through his own photographs and rummaging through magazines, books, and brochures—cutting out every image he could find of indigenous people, icons, symbols, art, architecture, and folk artifacts of the places he had been and the places he still wanted to go. Over the next year, he made 30 incredibly precise, culturally accurate, and spiritually inspiring montages of the world as he had come to know and understand it. Though most of his knowledge of these places was first hand, he did arduous research to confirm his intuitive understanding, extending his knowledge and authority, in many cases, to a world-class level. Peter felt that each montage had captured the soul of the people, places, and cultures he loved. He began to give talks using them to teach others what he had not been able to glean from his mainstream education.

> *Change and growth take place when a person has risked himself and dares to become involved with experimenting with his own life.*
>
> Herbert Otto

As a result of these talks, Peter became one of the very first cultural tour guides taking small groups of people on seat-of-your-pants, educational, cultural, and in-depth journeys to remote and primitive locations. Each of these tours greatly expanded Peter's understanding, passion, and now sizable collection of cultural artifacts. At the end of this twenty-year period, Peter once again returned to his original passion to depict the common themes in each of these cultures. This time, however, he chose to increase his canvas size from 16" x 20" collages to museum-style exhibits using all that he had collected over the previous forty-odd years of travel. With his montages as a graphic representation, Peter designed a dozen interactive environments that compose what he now envisions as an immersive, educational introduction to the great cultures of the world. Peter envisions "The World Memory Theater" as a traveling museum exhibit that represents what he believes to be the higher education he himself had spent years looking for.

Prodigy Practice #22 – Higher Education: Step outside the box to liberate the prodigy.

- Acknowledge Your Benefactors

The Hindus pay tribute to their masters, the Japanese build shrines, and Westerners dedicate schools and monuments. Prodigies read the biographies of their benefactors, imitate their styles, study their techniques, and view their accomplishments as mythic. They want to know how their benefactors struggled with the difficulties and obstacles in their path and ultimately achieved mastery. By engaging in this inquiry, prodigies receive a benediction from their benefactors.

The prodigy must be free to ask questions and seek guidance either directly or indirectly from his or her benefactors. The composer asks himself, "What chords would Beethoven play?"; the professor, "What would Plato say about this?"; the golfer, "What would Jack Nicklaus do?" Having a goal and a benefactor not only helps you prioritize the tasks before you, but it also bestows a respect for the path and a realistic understanding of what it takes to embody your gift.

Prodigy Story:

My son Elijah has always been the kind of person who likes to learn things on his own. It wasn't until he became a sushi chef that he began to value other people's knowledge. Though he chose not to go to culinary school, he knew the best way to accelerate his learning was to befriend the most talented chefs at each of the places he worked. For the first four years of his career, Elijah worked at various sushi bars specializing in what he disparagingly calls "white boy sushi." Though there were chefs at each of these restaurants with a degree of mastery, it wasn't until he got a job working for an "old-school" sushi chef that he truly learned the value of having a benefactor.

> *Many times a day I realize how much my own inner and outer life is built on the labors of other men, both living and dead, and how earnestly I must exert myself in order to give in return as much as I have received.*
>
> Albert Einstein

Strangely, the old-school sushi bar was one we used to eat at when Elijah was just five years old. The chef, who had served us twenty years before, was now Elijah's boss. Being Japanese and very traditional, Yoshi was reserved and considered that praise was not to be given lightly. Since Elijah believed he was already on his way to being a first-class sushi chef, he found working for Yoshi not only frustrating but an enormous blow to his ego. Elijah, accustomed to generous praise in his prior positions, now found himself working for a man who not only refused to acknowledge any of his efforts but, to make matters worse, his new boss never even referred to him by name.

Though he felt unseen and undervalued, Elijah couldn't deny the fact that he was learning more about his trade watching this quiet master out of the corner of his eye than he had learned from any of the other chefs with whom he had worked. For six months, Elijah worked tirelessly doing everything he could, attempting to master the subtleties Yoshi so effortlessly exhibited, hoping to win just a nod of approval for his skills and commitment.

One day Elijah was at the end of his rope and ready to quit. After many months of working without any recognition, he walked into work, silently nodded to his boss as he had everyday before, and was met for the first time with the earth shattering recognition he yearned, a nod and a barely audible greeting, "Elijah-san." All his hard worked had finally earned him the respect of a man he had grown to admire as a true master of a craft that was over a thousand years old. Beyond letting Elijah know, in his incredibly simple way, that he respected his work ethic and skills, Elijah was surprised to discover that he felt Yoshi had conferred upon him an initiation into a sacred lineage. With one simple acknowledgement, the master became his benefactor.

Soon after this happened, Elijah was re-offered his prior job at the most popular sushi bar in his town. Armed with a deep reverence for his craft and his lineage and a newfound respect for how much more he had left to learn, Elijah accepted the job. Several years have passed, but to this day when Elijah has a question regarding the art and craft of his lineage, he has a conversation in his mind with his otherwise restrained benefactor and receives the guidance and clarity he needs.

Prodigy Practice #23 – Walk With Your Benefactor: Identify your personal benefactor.

CHAPTER 7

Principle #5:

INTENTION ACTIVATES INTUITION INTUITION GENERATES INTENTION

Prodigies have a master plan that is not based on other people's realities but instead on the interface between their intuition, intention, and personal destiny. They are directed by a powerful sense of what is right for them. Though most respect the past, they believe it is their calling to invent the future. As a result of their commitment to following their intuition, prodigies are willing to take enormous risks, experiment with new techniques and technologies, devise unique approaches to confusing feedback, and above all, remain focused on their primary intention. When confronted with obstacles they intuitively prioritize the essentials, course correct, and pay attention to the results of their actions. There is a method to their madness, even if they don't always (consciously) know what it is. It's not that they embrace change more willingly than the rest of us; it's that, as their intention to succeed increases so does their intuition, while their willingness to be deterred (or detoured) tends to decrease exponentially.

By committing to your intentions, you effectively eliminate the meddlesome middleman—thinking. In other words if you try to think your way through a situation or problem, your solution will always be limited to the information you are already aware of, whereas if you hold the intention to discover the best solution, the necessary information and steps will be presented to you as you need them. Of the prodigies I've researched most make little distinction between an intention (the strongly held expectation that something will come to pass) and their intuition (the "feeling" or "sense" about what they need to do to help it happen). Your intention activates your intuition when you

> *Live as you will have wished to have lived when you are dying.*
>
> Christian Gellert

1) Develop a reliable channel of communication with your prodigy within

2) Act on the priceless insights and information it offers you

3) Observe the outcome of your actions and make the necessary course corrections.

By sensing what you want to do, setting a very clear intention to do it, and then observing what shows up, you create a perfect opportunity to recognize the difference between intuition, desire, antiquated beliefs and your destructive or delusional tendencies.

Werner Erhart, the founder of the est training, once said, "If you want to know what you intended, look what you got." If you discover that you don't get what you intend, then it's critical to identify the reason for the breakdown in the chain of command between your prodigy and your ability to recognize its voice. Perhaps you were not aligned with your intuition or you did not actually want what you were going after. By following the method of intending, intuiting, acting, and observing the result, the weak link in the chain of manifesting the prodigy's intention is revealed, refined, and actuated. In turn, when you follow your intuition and your intention manifests, you gain trust and clarity regarding your intuitive ability. This process results in honing your capacity to receive subtler and more precise intuitive information and commit more fully to your prodigy's intention.

- Benevolent Intent - Future Memory, Future Self

Benevolent intent affirms that throughout your life, in all decisions, victories, failures, aborted efforts, and realized dreams, there has been a presence—an intelligence—guiding you on your journey. Plato called it the Daimon, Christians refer to it as the Guardian Angel and others address it as their Higher Power. Whatever its name, it functions as benevolent intent. It is the voice, the hand, and the spirit of your prodigy within. It is future memory, working in the here and now. Though it often leads you to confront painful feelings, face selfish and unloving character traits, and re-enact disturbing dramas, its purpose is to help you emerge from the undergrowth of confusion, arrogance, and self-imposed exile. The recognition of the purifying presence of benevolent intent leads you to identify it as the positive, motivating force behind your intuitions. When this occurs, you're able to distinguish your intuition from fear, folly or ego. As you come to recognize the presence of benevolent intent, the gap between sensing and acting becomes negligible. Intuition generates intention, which effortlessly translates into action. Over time your decisions and actions organically align with benevolent intent and you find yourself consistently traveling on the "path of least resistance."

When you're in this groove and everything seems to be going your way, you are probably enjoying a deep level of communion with your prodigy. If, however, you begin to feel stuck or lost, getting back to the "path of least resistance" only requires that you ask the prodigy within for guidance, pay attention to what immediately shows up, and take the appropriate actions to support the forces of benevolent intent. In the story of Parsifal and the search for the Holy Grail as long as Parsifal asked the question, "How may I be of service?" he was guided through perilous adventures. When he stopped asking the question and decided he knew what was best, he found himself lost in the wilderness, without a clue! As he wandered through the desolate plague-ridden land, the suffering of humanity touched his heart and sparked his desire to be of service. It was this awakening followed by his commitment to be of service that activated the power of benevolent intent and lead Parsifal to the discovery of the Holy Grail. The Holy Grail, also known as the Cup of Destiny, is our life's purpose, our calling. It is what each of us discovers when we listen to the prodigy within and allow ourselves to enjoy the invisible power of benevolent intent.

Prodigy Story:

I hadn't seen Michael in ten years when he walked into the café where I was writing this book—talk about benevolent intent! I couldn't believe the difference in him. He looked thinner, healthier, and ten years younger, but what was most striking was he looked really happy—the kind of happy I've come to recognize on the faces of those who have found their calling. When we sat down to talk, Michael shared the story of how he had gone from an unhappy burnt-out Mercedes mechanic to a happy, extremely grateful, physical therapist. For a couple of years, he had been experiencing a low-grade angst that gelled one day when he was lifting an engine out of a car and his back started to give out. In that moment of pain he knew he couldn't—and no longer wanted to—continue being a mechanic. Though he was sure there "had to be more to life than this," there had to be a way for him to earn a living doing something he loved and something that made a difference, he believed he had no real marketable skills to fall back on. It was at this point he fell to his knees, gazed up, and in his own words, asked the question, "What do you want for me?"

> *If we take care of the means the ends take care of themselves.*
>
> Gandhi

Almost immediately, benevolent intent kicked in. A friend called and suggested he get a massage for his back. Michael had just been through a costly divorce and complained to his friend that he couldn't afford it, "you know, with alimony and all." His friend told him he could get one at a local massage school for $30.00 so he decided to get the massage. On the table, he felt, "something was telling me, pushing me to find out more." Over the next several weeks, Michael got five massages. During and after each massage, he questioned the therapists about how the school worked, how they paid for it and whether or not they thought they could actually earn a living at it. His curiosity was satisfied. Michael signed up for the school's payment plan though he still had no idea how he was going to come up with the money to pay for the course. But what he did know was it was calling him. He worked days at his garage, where business mysteriously picked up, and at nights attended classes. In every free moment, he gave family and friends free massages. Though he wasn't charging anything, tips were good. Miraculously, each time a payment was due at school, he had exactly what he needed (he didn't know about benevolent intent at the time). Michael's dedication and the power of his intention got him through his 150 hours of training in less time than any other student ever had and, to his surprise, when he tallied all of his tips, they added up to $1,500—the exact amount of the tuition.

> *Did you ever observe to whom the accidents happent? Chance favors only the prepared mind.*
>
> Louis Pasteur

From that point on Michael felt "everything fell into place, everything was too good to be true." He got a job at a health club doing massages and within six months was earning 50% of his income from massage and 50% as a mechanic. A client from the club who was a chiropractor invited Michael to partner with him. Within a couple months, Michael was earning 65% of his income from massage. He finally felt it was time to trust what was happening (benevolent intent) and give up working on cars completely. Days later, the chiropractor told Michael patients had been asking him if Michael could make house calls. Michael told the chiropractor he had been approached on a number of occasions as well but felt it was "inappropriate" and dismissed the offers. The chiropractor suggested if Michael were willing to give him $15.00 from each massage, he would happily refer his patients. It took Michael a couple of months and he was earning considerably more than he had been generating as a full-time mechanic.

After a couple of months building his private practice, Michael found himself facing what looked like the end of his massage career.

Over a two-week period his hands began to swell and developed a rash. He went to doctors, tried every kind of pharmaceutical and home remedy available, but to no avail. He was heartbroken to have finally found his calling only to have it snatched away when the brass ring was finally within his grasp. But, once again, the unseen hand of benevolent intent delivered him a miracle.

A client who had become dependent on Michael's healing hands called for an appointment and Michael explained to him why he would be unable to see him. The client suggested a trip to Hawaii might help, bought Michael a ticket, and invited him to stay at his beachfront home. Michael accepted the generous offer. While there, he spent hours floating in the ocean, enjoying the scenery, and contemplating his next move. To Michael's surprise, within two days his hands cleared up. Apparently some kind of microorganism in the water, indigenous to Hawaii, had provided the cure for his hands. Michael bottled up several gallons of the water, returned to the mainland and to his work, and was soon enjoying another enormous leap in his earnings.

Michael's experience has changed him profoundly. He has come to accept that as long as his intentions are pure, his way will be guided and opportunities will continue to unfold that are far greater than anything he could dream for himself. Michael now knows that by listening to his intuition and acting in alignment with his intentions, benevolent intent functions as his business coach in every decision he has to make.

Prodigy Practice #24 – Future Memory: Collaborate with Your Higher Power.

- Rules Were Made to Be Broken

When Frank Sinatra sang, "I Did It My Way," he was unabashedly identifying the source of his success. Prodigies achieve greatness because they march (or dance) to the beat of their own drummer. Beethoven wasn't dissuaded from using dissonant chord progressions in his compositions just because no one had done it before him. Had he listened to the wisdom of the day, espoused by the great composer Handel, he would never have revolutionized music. If Einstein had believed Newton was the final word on physics, he would never have discovered the Theory of Relativity. Georgia O'Keeffe believed before she could really express what she felt and saw she had to forget all the rules she had learned about painting. Thomas Jefferson, Susan B. Anthony, and Babe Ruth are names we remember because they all did it their way.

> *Einstein continued to work hard at his physics until the end. The curious thing was, he worked in complete disagreement with almost all of his contemporaries.*
>
> *"New Statesman"*
>
> C.P. Snow

When I look into my life and recall the people I regard as prodigies, without fail every one of them found their own way to accomplish their unique strategy for success. "Rules were made to be broken" means always looking for your way to manifest your calling. When you are committed to doing it your way, you throw open the floodgates of insight and intuition. Since there has never been another person with your particular constellation of strengths, talents and desires, you cannot expect to follow a precise formula. The path to fulfilling your calling is what Carlos Castaneda, author and shaman to the baby boom generation, referred to as a "path with heart." Only when you are fully committed to your heart's path will you have the strength to break the rules that have kept you a slave to an unfulfilling job, fear-based decisions, and your dearly held attachment to how unique you are or are not. A "path with heart" is a path that is not buried under half-truths and half-hearted efforts to be true to your prodigy within.

Prodigy Story:

At the age of 52, Katrina had raised her children, taught martial arts, been a bodyguard for various celebrities (male and female), and worked as a real estate agent and mortgage broker. Other than her role as a mother, Katrina had never felt that she was living her own life. When we first began talking about who she wanted to be when she grew up, all she could remember were the plans her father had for her future. With tears in her eyes Katrina recalled, "My father had always wanted a boy, and I did everything I possibly could to be what he wanted. Though he said otherwise, I always knew what a disappointment I was to him. I remember wanting to please my father so badly that at my first karate tournament I made such a stink about how unfair it was that I couldn't compete against the boys that my father threatened to sue the federation. When I won my division by kicking the best boy's ass, it was the proudest moment of my life. It was also probably the beginning of the end of knowing what Katrina wanted for another 30 years."

> *Hell, there are no rules here—we're trying to accomplish something.*
>
> Thomas A. Edison

After spending most of her life trying to make it in a man's world, Katrina arrived in her fifties dissatisfied, filled with remorse, and consumed by terrible feelings of anger and emptiness. After doing a number of the Prodigy Practices Katrina discovered her real passion was to be "some kind of a healer." She decided to undertake a six-month experiment that included leaving her lucrative mortgage banker position, researching various healing modalities, and taking a job at a small retail store specializing in Chinese herbs. When she told her father, ex-husband, and business partner, they laughed out loud telling her she was crazy and this was probably the stupidest thing she had ever done. Though their words and laughter pierced her heart, Katrina could no longer be deterred from seeking her own path.

> *Alter your habits and you alter your character and thus your fate.*
>
> *"Soul's Code"*
>
> James Hillman

It took only a couple of weeks at her new $10.00 an hour job to convince Katrina she was following her calling. By living in sync with her Archetypes of Service (Healer, Altruist and Problem Solver), she was experiencing a joy and satisfaction she had never before known. For the first time since childhood, she was tireless, consuming every book she could find, experimenting on herself and her friends, and researching every imaginable kind of healing school to find a certification program that "rang her chimes." Within a couple of months, she was enrolled in college to secure an undergraduate degree; she had decided upon a homeopathic college that felt like a perfect fit. Even after graduating from college with a Bachelor of Science degree, the laughter and derisive comments continued. Though she was experiencing a profound sense of purpose and well being, she recognized the rules that remained to be broken were the ones she had internalized from a lifetime of trying to be someone other than who she really was. With the confidence that accompanied every step toward fulfilling her calling, Katrina wrote a new rulebook.

I saw Katrina recently, for the first time in two years. She looked like a completely different person. The mask she used to wear had evaporated and her real self was shining through loud and clear. She was practicing homeopathy under the license of a masterful homeopathic doctor, seeing 15-20 clients a week, enjoying her day job prescribing Chinese herbs and living a life that she had never imagined was possible. When I asked her if I could use her as an example of Rules Were Made to Be Broken, she agreed, commenting that her passion to become a homoeopathist had led her to discover in herself an additional Archetype of Service, The Activist. She then went on to speak in detail about her passion to change the laws that limit the practice of homeopathy, "a science based on the same principles Jonas Salk employed in his Nobel Prize-winning discovery of the Salk vaccine."

When we said goodbye, Katrina laughed at the irony of my asking her to be an example of Rules Were Made to Be Broken. "You know, after a life of living for others, I love having discovered how much joy I get thumbing my nose at rules. Not only does it come into play in my profession, but as you know, an Activist lives to discover rules that need to be broken."

Prodigy Practice #25 – Sacred Cows: Identify beliefs that interfere with your intuition.

- To Thine Own Prodigy Be True

As we liberate ourselves from our unconscious limitations, we become free, maybe for the first time ever, to hear and be true to our own prodigy. "If your primary responsibility in life is being true to yourself, that can only be accomplished by carrying out what you are called to do—your unique and special vocation" (author Dennis

Kimbro, Ph.D.). In order to merge the intuition with intention, you must commit yourself to doing only what rings true for you in your heart and mind. For most of us this is a tall order, contrary to years of education, parental expectations, and the prevailing belief that the shortest distance between two points is to sacrifice who you are and what you feel so you can receive a huge payoff later which will allow you to finally do what you want—which, of course, entails following your feelings and being who you really are. The price paid for this kind of delusional "sacrifice" is the deep erosion of your trust in your own innate wisdom, the prodigy within. A lifetime of abandoning the prodigy not only destroys our intuition, it also undermines our ability to fulfill the prodigy's intentions and purpose. Over time, our true calling is buried beneath a lifetime of choices based on survival, ego, and fear. Not until we practice being true to thine own prodigy do we begin to release our innate wisdom, the prodigy within, that leads us to our calling.

> *To thine own self be true.*
> *Therefore like the night*
> *that follows the day you*
> *can be false to no man.*
>
> Shakespeare

The road to reestablishing a deep, respectful, and enlightened relationship with the prodigy requires us to...

1. Turn within.
2. Seek guidance.
3. Take the internally prescribed action.
4. Observe the results with an open, non-judgmental attitude.

When we approach our intuition in this way, even when it proves erroneous or misguided, it offers us an extraordinary opportunity to rehabilitate our relationship with the prodigy. For example, let's say you believe you've intuited the direction in which your prodigy is guiding you to take, you invest your intention by taking the appropriate actions and when it's all said and done, you feel you ended up a million miles away from where you thought you were headed. Now, even though you didn't end up at the destination you "thought" you'd intuited, you have generated an opportunity to 1) educate yourself to your tendencies; 2) distinguish the unique voice of your intuition from all of the other voices that reside in your head; and 3) begin to mend the long-standing rift between your intuition and your intentions.

By looking to discover how you attempt to follow your intuition, you create an extraordinary opportunity to generate the kind of precise insights that will heal and strengthen the power of your intention. The insights you uncover might reveal that you're easily distracted by innate fears, misguided by the machinations of your mind or possessed by your subconscious tendencies to do the same thing over and over again with the expectation of different results. Whatever is revealed through your willingness to practice this level of self-reflection, the payoff is always an enormous step toward the merging of intuition and intention.

Two young women from America who wanted to study with Matisse in Paris said, "We want your color" to which he replied, "Schools and things that painters taught me kept me from painting as I wanted to. I decided that I was a very stupid fool not to say what I wanted to say when I painted.

Henri Matisse

What, exactly, arises in you that results in selling out your dreams? Is it fear, over consideration, setting unrealistic goals, comparing yourself to others, perfectionism, demoralizing internal dialogue or a negative core belief of insufficiency or unworthiness? Avoid judging yourself for any of these: just commit yourself to identifying your sell-out triggers, in all their permutations. Remember, knowledge is power and we are only controlled by those thoughts, beliefs and feelings whose existence we are unconscious of. By becoming conscious of your tendency to abandon your true self, you make way for the energy locked up in habitual patterns to be released, washing away old habits like a storm-fed stream cleansing its banks. The blockages, one after another, are washed away in the torrent of awareness. This conscious free-flowing energy initiates and sustains the unraveling of lifelong karmic patterns. These karmic patterns, knots of memory based on past events that we are unaware of and have not forgiven ourselves for, are liberated from the mind and body as we learn to be true to our own prodigy.

> *Schools and things that painters taught me kept me from painting as I wanted to. I decided that I was a very stupid fool not to say what I wanted to say when I painted.*
>
> Georgia O'Keeffe

As a yoga teacher, I often remind people to observe what it is they do to abandon the moment. Using the yogic technique of focusing the awareness on the breath, we flow through a continuous fluid stream of challenging physical postures. Inevitably all students lose track of their breath, and thus abandon the present moment. Some students push too hard and get caught up in trying. Others don't push at all and tend to get lulled into complacency. Others still try to do each posture perfectly, wonder what the next posture might be or check out how much better their neighbor's practice is than theirs. All of these tendencies accomplish the same goal—abandonment of the now, of one's intentions and, of course, one's self. By continuously observing, without judgment or criticism, their tendencies in the controlled environment of their yoga practice, the yoga students begin to learn how they abandon their self in life. Just like the yogi, each of us must discover how we sell out the prodigy within. We must practice being present and thus resurrect the life we were born to live.

Prodigy Story:

I had been working in the fields of health and holistic medicine for many years when I stumbled into a position as creative director for a non-profit educational foundation. In this position I was responsible for overseeing large-scale events that came under the banner of edutainment (educational entertainment). This position opened my eyes to the transformative power of entertainment and catalyzed for my desire to study filmmaking. I graduated from film school and experimented in various areas of filmmaking: documentaries, television, interactive CD-ROM's and special effects. I discovered the world of special effects felt most closely aligned with my purpose, to create immersive, transformative and spiritually uplifting experiences, so I veered toward specialty films and theme park entertainment.

Through a friend, I was introduced to an organization that hired me as creative director for a large theme park in Singapore. It was the "opportunity of a lifetime," as all my friends constantly reminded me, yet I had a steady churning in my gut whenever I drove the twenty miles to work to prepare for my move to Singapore. Outwardly there was no explanation as to why I felt this sense of dread. As time passed, the churning only grew stronger; I tried to shake it off, but the feeling persisted. I was stumped and decided to dismiss my feelings as simply fear of failure.

A week left before I had to sign the final contract, I went to visit my minister, Reverend Michael Beckwith, to try one last time to get to the bottom of my feelings. After listening carefully to my story Reverend Michael said one thing, "There are no lost opportunities." Now this may not seem particularly earth shattering or insightful, but it was all it took for me to give myself permission to "follow my gut" and back out of the "opportunity of a lifetime." I immediately felt an incredible sense of relief. Three weeks later, my real "opportunity of a lifetime" arrived in the form of a job to design pavilions, rides, films, and exhibits for the World's Fair in South Korea. In this position I was free to exercise more of my skills, gifts, and passions than ever before. I designed, created and produced dozens of immersive, uplifting experiences. For the first time in my life, I felt conscious of my own distinctive way of giving and confident about my unique constellation of talents. Above all, I learned to trust my gut and be true to the prodigy within to the point that I now rarely question the authenticity of my feelings, guidance or calling.

Prodigy Practice #26 – Selling Out: Identify how you abandon the prodigy within.

- Play With Your Food

In one of the most memorable scenes from Steven Spielberg's film, *Close Encounters of the Third Kind*, the lead character, driven by an unconscious inspiration transmitted to him by the aliens, plays with his mashed potatoes. As he sits at the dining room table, oblivious to his family screaming around him, he literally plays with his food. As he mindlessly forks the mashed potatoes, his higher mind (the prodigy) shapes the potatoes into a mountain. We see the same struggle among the other key characters as they attempt to transform their inspiration into understanding. Some sculpt it, others draw it, and still others receive it as a musical melody. All of the people play, stumble and allow themselves to be guided. As the movie progresses, we discover the music and mountain represent the call and location of an alien visitation. The process depicted in the film demonstrates the precise way we invite the prodigy to reveal the intuitions and inspirations it has to share with us as guidance.

The ability to play with our food is one of the most distinguishable characteristics of prodigies. Though prodigies are often thought of as serious and hard working, they are not limited by the rigid rules the rest of us seek comfort in. Even though they may not know exactly where they're going, they'll try anything that strikes their fancy in order to channel their vision and attain their hearts desire. Though others often believe prodigies can be indulgent, misguided and oft times ridiculous, it is this very attribute of willingness they have to play with their food that results in their successes and distinguishes them from those who judge them. Prodigies' healthy disdain for what others think about them allows them to experiment continuously with unique ways of doing things, and risk making "fools" of themselves, if necessary.

> *A child-like adult is not one whose development is arrested; on the contrary, he is an adult who has given himself a chance of continuing to develop long after most people have muffled themselves into a cocoon of middle age habit and convention.*
>
> Aldous Huxley

For most of us, it's easy to get trapped in the pursuit of our goals with a zeal that blinds us to the infinite realm of possibilities that lay before us. We sacrifice the willingness to play, experiment, and practice a devil-may-care attitude, which may cut us off from the active guidance of our prodigy and the passive opportunities that flow to us through benevolent intent.

So go ahead: cut it up, turn it on its ear, make it fun, add a healthy dose of chaos, flirt with the ludicrous, play with your food.

Prodigy Story:

Perhaps one of the most famous examples of someone who found his way, later in life, by playing with his food, was Jackson Pollock, the quintessential abstract expressionist. Pollock had been a serious student of art who was trained at the best schools in the classical techniques of representational painting. He stumbled along for years painting what he was told would sell. After many years of "banging his head," he began to feel maybe he should abandon his passion. He knew that he had taken the style and technique of traditional painting as far as he could. He felt that he had reached a dead end and he was no longer being true to himself trying to work within the "Agreement Reality," (what is collectively believed to be real, good or true), what others believed art was suppose to look like. In his frustration Pollock, believing he had nothing to lose, gave himself permission to express what he felt, to play with his food, so to speak. When he began to throw, drizzle, and slap paint onto canvas, he wasn't thinking, he was stumbling into his personal style. He himself said about this process, "I have no fears about mak-

> *When you create you lose yourself in your own knowing, and come back with an idea, a feeling, a character, a better mousetrap.*
>
> *"The Creativity Book"*
>
> *Eric Maisel*

ing changes, destroying the image … because the painting has a life of its own."

By playing with his food, venting his pain, anger and frustration and perhaps being prodded, just a little, by his prodigy within, Jackson Pollock uncovered his calling. As we know, Jackson Pollock's willingness to play with his food resulted in his becoming the highest paid artist of his day and revolutionizing, not without considerable controversy (even to this day), the agreement reality regarding what is and isn't art. Among many art critics, he is considered the second most influential painter (behind another painter who played with his food, Pablo Picasso) of the 20th century. Pollock would never have established his revered position of "destroying all that is good in art" (depending whom you talk to); arrived as the "father of abstract expressionism"; or discovered his true calling if he had not been willing to play with his food.

Prodigy Practice #27 – Play Daze: Let the spirit of play give your prodigy a voice.

• Embracing Intentional Awareness – Learning to Stop, Look, Listen and Reflect

Learning to stop, look and listen is an acquired skill; developing the intention to do so and awareness of the practice is the first step. When asked how he came up with his famous theorems, Einstein said he wasn't smarter than others, only more inquisitive and more attentive. Ideas, inspiration, and opportunities surround us. By defining your intention and focusing it as the lens through which you view the world, everything you do and everything that comes your way has the potential to reveal insights, truths and new directions.

As you exercise your intentional awareness, it expands exponentially, flooding your conscious mind with a steady stream of guidance, nourishment and revelation. Over time your confidence and reliance upon your intuition—the voice of your prodigy within—increases and takes over as your primary tool for navigation toward your calling.

It's important to note that there is one critical factor that always interferes with our ability to embrace intentional awareness—our aptitude for distinguishing our intuitions from all of the other voices that rattle around in our head. I identify the critical factor that prevents us from trusting our intuition (the voice of the prodigy) as the unquestioned beliefs we unconsciously subscribe to. These "agreement realities" include those things we individually and collectively believe to be descriptions of and laws regarding how the world is and should be. Things like

- What we believe to be possible
- How we think things should be done
- What constitutes appropriate and inappropriate behavior
- How we define what a responsible adult should do or be
- What we expect the outcome of our efforts to be
- What we identify as possible and impossible

By being unconscious of the agreement reality we subscribe to, we limit ourselves from new ways of seeing and experiencing the world. We also lose out on the enormous range of opportunities that arrive via benevolent intent. For example, one agreement reality many of us have unconsciously bought into is that work is equated with sacrificing pleasure, bearing a burden, and doing things you wouldn't do if you didn't have to. It's obvious if you subscribe to this agreement reality consciously or unconsciously, you are not going to be open and available to the possibility of doing work that's fun, easy and something you really love doing. When we are limited by our unconscious agreement reality we are 1) unavailable to the sacred utterances of the prodigy that arrive via the intuition; and 2) incapable of believing that intentions that conflict with our beliefs about how things are could ever manifest. When you become willing to question the agreement reality you have adopted as your truth, you begin to dissolve their limiting effects in your life and become available to practicing and embracing intentional awareness.

THE 7 STEPS TO INTENTIONAL AWARENESS

1. Commit to an intention. Intend to receive an intuition. Focus on it being attracted into your life. Hold it in your heart. Trust it will be revealed to you.

2. Stop, look and listen to the constant flow of information and opportunities streaming into your life.

3. Consider what shows up as an extension of your intention.

4. Acknowledge the dramatic increase in feelings, synergy and synchronicity as guidance, leading you to where you should go, what you should do; and when you should wait.

5. Take the appropriate actions.

6. Observe the results.

7. Consult your intuition for what's next by noticing what you're now intending.

Prodigy Story:

A dear friend of mine, Lee, has earned his living as a master carpenter for nearly 40 years. In fact, up until recently, Lee believed carpentry to be his calling. In the last few years, however, Lee's 54-year-old body began to rebel against all the years of hard physical labor. Simultaneously, as so often happens, he began yearning "to be of greater service and be financially supported doing it."

Though Lee is an exceptional carpenter, he is a truly gifted spiritual teacher. When we first met I lovingly nicknamed him The Preacher. Though Lee is not earning his living as a spiritual counselor, almost every person in his life recognizes it as his calling and responds accordingly by seeking his insights and guidance. For over 20 years Lee has led ongoing groups (for fun and for free) based on a spiritual study program known as the Science of Mind. Without any formal education or degrees, Lee's passion and commitment to share what has served and transformed him has made him a trusted spiritual adviser to hundreds of grateful people.

> *Isn't it astonishing that all these secrets have been preserved for so many years just so we could disver them!*
>
> Orville Wright

In an attempt to use his carpentry skills as a stepping stone toward aligning his work and his true passion, his spiritual life, Lee began to entertain the idea of creating a business designing, building and marketing a line of prefab sacred spaces to be used as studios, retreats, and sanctuaries. Though Lee didn't focus daily on his intention to earn his living building sacred spaces, his daily activities were always clearly and unequivocally engaged in embracing his intention to create a sacred space wherever he was, whatever he was doing. As a result of Lee's powerful intention and unwavering commitment, benevolent intent always tended to guide Lee to the right people, places and opportunities to be of service and expand his calling

Soon after Lee began scribbling drawings of sacred spaces and speaking of his desire to create them, he got a job building an "exercise studio" for an extremely wealthy couple. For over six months Lee worked tirelessly, without the slightest acknowledgement from the couple. At one point, when the structure was nearly complete, the wife, a somewhat obsessive attorney, came by to examine the progress and recognized, for the first time, the extraordinary quality of Lee's craftsmanship. Seeing the workmanship allowed her to "see" Lee for the first time as well. Over the next few weeks the previously cold and distant couple began to warm toward Lee. It was during this time the mutual friend who had recommended Lee to the couple told them about his weekly Science of Mind group. The husband, suffering from leukemia, asked Lee if he would be willing to start another group in the now complete exercise studio. The following week Lee began teaching Science of Mind in what the wife had begun to refer to as "the sanctuary." Every Thursday for the next several months, Lee shared the principles of the Science of Mind teachings with the couple, their highly dysfunctional family, and a group of friends and employees. The combination of Lee's spiritual teachings, the magic of "the sanctuary" and the family's receptiveness initiated a healing among the family and friends. Though Lee was still not earning his living from his calling, the couple went out of their way to create building projects at their numerous properties to keep Lee and his "uplifting presence" in their lives. When the couple learned Lee and his fiancé Francis were searching for a suitable location for their wedding ceremony, they lovingly and unconditionally offered "the estate and the sanctuary," a gift worth many thousands of dollars.

Several months after the wedding, the husband's health took a turn for the worse. In the grip of fear and despair, the couple turned once again to Lee to minister to the family's needs and to Francis to share her healing gifts with the husband. What had begun as a Science of Mind study group evolved into Lee and Francis facilitating the healing of a family that had been divided by anger, rife with resentment, and torn by feelings repressed for over 20 years. With Lee and Francis's help, the couple mended their relationships with their estranged children, something no one in their extended family ever believed possible. Truths were spoken, tears were shed, and resentments were released. As the grateful recipients of a "miracle beyond words," the family once again generously gifted Lee and Francis, this time monetarily, for their unwavering commitment and tireless efforts in facilitating the healing of the ancient wounds that had destroyed their health, their lives and their family. Lee and Francis were overwhelmed by the extraordinary generosity of the gift and the family's effusive expressions of love that accompanied it. Though neither Lee nor Francis considered the gift wages, it far exceeded what Lee would have earned in the same period of time as a builder and has allowed him to continue "ministering." Their experience has left both of them with the indelible impression—that following their hearts is their calling.

Though Lee has no idea how his intention to earn his living as a spiritual counselor will manifest next, he knows that no matter what happens he's taken a step out of his old life into a new life that feels safe, supported, and divinely inspired. As Lee continues to embrace the intention to create sacred spaces, he has no attachment or illusions as to whether or not he will ever actually construct a physical structure as the embodiment of his intention. He does, however, know without any doubt that the universe hears his prayers, answers them accordingly and only asks of him that he keep his eyes, ears and heart open to recognizing the miraculous way they manifest.

Prodigy Practice #28 – Embracing Intentional Awareness: Practice intending.

- Sixth Sensing

What is sixth sensing? It is the ability to know, without sustaining logic, scientific proof or external agreement. When prodigies are asked why they took a specific, seemingly irrational action that resulted in a "Eureka!" moment, they almost always respond by saying, "I just knew it was the right thing to do." Though there are numerous books on the subject, developing your sixth sense is best summed up in the saying intuition follows intention. That's why, when blocked, the irrepressible commitment prodigies have often results in an attitude shift that mysteriously activates their sixth sense. When this happens, they find themselves in the stream of consciousness where intuitive insights and serendipitous events bring them the clarity they require to manifest their intention. To those on the outside these inexplicable occurrences are dismissed as luck rather than what they are—the universe organizing a solution and direction in response to the prodigy's intentional commitment to living their calling.

> *Noah listened to the voice within, the voice of benevolent intent and built an ark, (a boat in the middle of the desert.)*
>
> *"Building Your Field of Dreams"*
> Mary Manin Morrissey

Prodigy Story:

In the 1880s, Thomas Edison was working on 44 inventions all at one time, including the telegraph, submarine cable, sound measuring instruments, mimeographs, telephone, incandescent light, and various drugs and chemicals. For each of these inventions he had an assistant who was in charge of moving Edison's intentions and inventions toward a successful resolution. Each day Edison walked around from assistant to assistant with unchecked curiosity to discuss their progress and make course corrections. Just as he meandered around his lab from one assistant to the next, so too he meandered around in his mind to uncover the next step, phase or experiment that would eventually lead him to perfecting the invention at hand. Edison himself understood this process perfectly. "Look, I start here with the intention of going there. But when I have arrived part way in my straight line, I meet with a phenomenon, and it leads me off in a direction to something totally unexpected."

In his book, "Edison: A Biography," Matthew Josephson offers the example of how, after visiting an assistant, Edison would retreat to his library and pore through masses of books for hours on end. He'd simply allow himself to be guided toward books that he sensed might divulge new clarity, insight or a clear-cut direction. After this process of blue-skying (see below) he would return refreshed to his assistant and the problem at hand with a new sense of where to go and what to do next with the bolstered belief they were one step closer to success. It was Edison's sixth sense that guided him along untrodden paths toward the discovery and patents of hundreds of ground-breaking inventions and to the extraordinary impact his gift has had on modern life.

Prodigy Practice #29 – Blue Skying: Free the subconscious, activate your intuition.

CHAPTER 8

Principle #6: INHABIT A SENSE OF DIVINE URGENCY

Prodigies have a Sense of Divine Urgency regarding their personal destiny. Many times this translates into the feeling that if they don't do what they have to do, it will never be done and the world will be the poorer for it. They live with the awareness that they only have so much time and can't afford to waste it. They are willing to make enormous sacrifices (comfort, wealth, relationship, etc.), foregoing many of the luxuries and pleasant distractions others feel they can't live without. Though they have a sense of divine urgency, it rarely translates into sloppiness, impatience or cutting corners. They are, for the most part, driven not from without, but motivated from within. They have tremendous enthusiasm. Unlike most of us, a prodigy's anger strengthens his or her resolve, resulting in additional motivation. Among late-blooming baby-boomers, the first awakening to a sense of divine urgency arrives when they become fed up with doing "work that has no meaning." This is followed by the need to make a real contribution and an obsession with the demoralizing reality that "if I don't do it now, I never will!"

What would it take to inspire you to Inhabit a Sense of Divine Urgency? The key is discovering a need that isn't being met (that has real meaning to you), holding the intention that you are blessed with the opportunity to meet that need and that you will be provided with the guidance required to do so. The more powerfully you resonate with that unmet need, the more compelling the call to respond with a Sense of Divine Urgency.

- If Not Now, When? If Not You, Who?

It's time to kick it up a notch. You can't understand why you're still feeling more like Sisyphus (you know the guy whose hell was pushing a boulder to within a millimeter of the top of a mountain with his nose, only to have it roll back down every time) than Sir Edmund Hillary heading to the top of Everest. You're showing up, you're practicing, you've got a mentor, and you probably even have a sixth sense about where you're going, but it still feels like you're not going anywhere. This is the time to make a decision about your priorities—a decision about what's most important to you and whether you're willing to do what it takes to achieve it. You can be sure that making this decision will likely generate an inexplicable level of resistance from friends, co-workers, and your subconscious mind. The people in our life who think they know who we are, who we are suppose to be, or what is best for us become very uncomfortable when we begin to grow, change and rock the status quo. When we threaten the agreement reality of those around us by charting our own course, they are inevitably roused to dissuade us from following our dreams by clouding our intention with fear, consideration, and threats. "You're wasting your time." "You're not being responsible." "Those are just pipe dreams, you're acting like a fool." "That's fine for teenagers but you've got to think of your family and your retirement." "Not at your age." "How will you earn a living" These are not the words of malicious people, but the words of people who have forsaken their own dream of discovering their calling. Your courage to step wholeheartedly into the Quest to discover your calling is experienced as a direct confrontation to those who haven't. Their attempt to derail you is nothing more than their need to avoid facing that abandonment of their Self and their life's purpose.

> *Courage is the by-product of communion rather than an individual virtue, the creation of a compassionate community rather than a psychological quality some people have and others lack.*
>
> *"Learning to Fly"*
>
> Sam Keen

When you have made the decision that this is the When and you are the Who, to do exactly what has been put in your heart and soul, then every aspect of your life will accelerate in the direction of your calling. A vector will travel through every situation, propelling you along the line of least resistance (though it may not feel that way). Your decision to trust that you are the Who and this is the When will generate a boldness that will propel you through blocks that used to paralyze you. Instead of struggling and limping along, you'll feel you are truly supported and guided. The sweet pleasure of knowing that you are the Who, this is the When and that you are supported in the What (your calling) will be undeniable.

Prodigy Story:

Mark spent his entire life trying to prove to his father, the atheist, that he was worthy of his love. He started several businesses from scratch, built them into successes, then sold them or drove them into the ground because, "they just weren't me. I was doing them for the money, for my father, my wife and family, but ultimately to avoid facing the fact that I didn't know who Mark was, let alone what he really wanted. I look back now and know that my lack of direction and fear were one of the main reasons I turned to drinking,"

> *The people who get on in this world are the people who get up and look for the circumstances they want, and, if they can't find them, make them.*
>
> George Bernard Shaw

In a haze of guilt, misplaced responsibility, and a need to prove he was lovable, Mark bounced around from stockbroker to mortgage banker. He built a printing business and created a window-washing franchise but had yet to discover what he wanted. Then he hit bottom in his drinking and his "house of cards" life came crashing down around him. His wife left, there were a couple of warrants for his arrest, his business failed, he couldn't find work and no one, including his own children, wanted anything to do with him. He was shattered and his shattering gave him the courage and determination to face himself, his past and the story he had adopted to support his feelings of being "good for nothing." Mark knew that NOW was finally the time to get real, look at himself and turn his life over. Mark made the decision and began asking God to show him how "I could be of service to my fellow humans." He jumped whole-heartedly into his Quest. It started with joining AA and getting sober. After a couple of years, Mark was sponsoring fifteen guys. Instead of focusing on himself he'd make a house call to someone whose wife just left him, bail a sponsee out of jail or spend an hour helping a guy who lost his job put his resume together. He joined a church and created a faith recovery program in the back rooms, where he found himself ministering to bikers, ex-cons, gang members and alimony dodgers. He cleaned up his debt, put a $100,000 in the bank and flew around the country to make face-to-face amends to everyone he had hurt. Mark experienced being trusted and respected once again, that he was valued for his supportive words and insights, and he was loved and therefore lovable. The joy he was receiving from giving his gift was something he wanted a lot more of. Though he didn't know exactly what was next, he knew that this was the When and he was the Who.

Mark, now 43, started praying for guidance to the best way to expand his calling. He prayed for a mentor. When Mark remembered the positive influence his own high school counselor had on him, he felt this would be his path and began looking for a college to enroll in to pursue a career in counseling. During this time, Mark's father became very sick, and Mark and his wife became his primary caretakers. Over the next couple of years, Mark healed his relationship to his father, and his father began to tell him (daily) how proud he was of him, how much he loved him, and through Mark's example even came to believe in God. While still involved in completing the courses he needed to get into the Master's program, his mentor appeared. It was, of all people, the pastor at his church. He trained Mark as an Elder and shortly thereafter offered Mark the position of Associate Pastor. Mark was stunned. He admired this man greatly and knew him to be extremely spiritual and insightful. He couldn't believe this man believed he was worthy to be a leader, but even more, that he was willing to entrust him with the spiritual care of his congregation.

Mark, confused and overwhelmed, went to his A.A. sponsor and father for advice. He asked his sponsor, "Why me?" She responded, "Why not you? Who has been better prepared? Who has done the work and prayed for this opportunity?" But ultimately, it was his father's words on his deathbed that convinced him. "Who better than you? Anyone lucky enough to have you guide them on their spiritual path will be blessed beyond compare. A few years ago you couldn't even spell the word integrity, now you walk it!" It was the proudest moment of Mark's life. In one moment, his father had given him what he had yearned for all of his life. Needless to say he accepted the position. Mark's new job included counseling, consoling those in grief, and helping young men and woman gain a firm footing on the path to achieving their life's dreams. Mark was so moved when he performed his first baptism and funeral that he describes them as peak experiences.

In our most recent conversation Mark told me, "Every day I live in amazement. I am so grateful to have this gift that some people never get."

"What is that?" I asked.

"That I am enough. It's not what I'm doing; it's knowing in the Lord's eyes I am more than enough. Everything I do now is an extension of finally knowing this great fact and believing it at the core of my being." After some more small talk, Mark, in his joyful and serene way, casually mentioned, "Oh, by the way, Curtis (his pastor) told me it's time for me to spread my wings." After a pause, tears rising up in his throat, Mark said, "He said it's time to become the pastor of my own congregation… Who would have ever thought?"

Prodigy Practice #30 – No Way Out: Define the Prodigy's "Hierarchy of Needs."

- Escape Velocity

The beginning of any endeavor is the hardest and most perilous part of the journey. Like rocket ships preparing for take off, most of us start things with an explosion, then stumble, lumber and stall. A rocket whose engines are straining against its mooring is closer to its promise to reach its destination than at any time since its conception as an idea. But, as it lumbers through the dense atmosphere, attempting to gain escape velocity (the momentum required to break free of the earth's gravitational field), the most energy intensive and tenuous phase of its entire journey threatens to deny it its goal. However once the spacecraft has pierced through the earth's atmosphere, its engines are cut off and it glides effortlessly through the vacuum of space at 17,000 mph.

> *Those who are victorious plan effectively and change decisively. They are like a great river that maintains its course but adjusts its flow.*
>
> Sun Tzu

Momentum is everything: the hardest thing to gain, the easiest to lose. How often have you set your sights on a goal you desperately wanted, designed an intelligent plan, and created a reasonable deadline, only to suddenly get a long-term visit from an in-law, a slew of unexpected bills, or a call from your last employer offering you your old job with a 25% raise. Any or all of these are perfectly legitimate excuses for being lured away from fulfilling the prodigy's intentions. The distasteful outcome of abandoning your prodigy is losing the momentum you struggled so hard to acquire, and tumbling back to earth in a blaze of anger and a shroud of self-pity.

Like any prodigy, you must learn to guard your time, focus, and momentum vigilantly to achieve escape velocity. Once you're no longer plagued by the gravitational pull of distraction and self-doubt, the prodigy is freer than ever to guide and inspire you. Once free of the shackles of old agreement realities, escape velocity transforms into forward momentum: the tendency to keep moving in the direction of your calling.

Prodigy Story:

Donna was married at 22. She spent the next 25 years, more or less happily, as a wife, mother of three, and homemaker. Prior to her marriage, she was as an aspiring segment producer on a top local newscast. Soon after her marriage, Donna was offered her "big break," producing a nationally syndicated game show. Professionally she had achieved escape velocity. Her husband, knowing she'd be flying free and their plans for a family delayed or derailed, presented her with The Ultimatum, "work or me." After some heart wrenching reflection, she capitulated and tumbled back to earth like so many women do when they choose family over work (and/or calling). Donna made her full-time job managing their large home, raising the children, and overseeing the family finances. But, her children grew up, her marriage began to erode, and she was suddenly facing questions about who she really was and if she had a calling beyond cooking dinner and raising children. At the time her children entered high school, Donna formulated a clear intention to discover her calling. Much to her surprise, when she shared her desire to find her purpose, her husband, children and friends ridiculed and criticized her. They were more concerned about her extra-familial activities interfering with their lives than her need to feed the part of herself that she felt was dying.

Fully aware of the resistance she would receive as she pursued her dream, Donna formulated a plan that would help her achieve "lift-off." She figured that as long as she was able to keep her family happy, she could do whatever she wanted and they wouldn't try to stop her. With her plan in place Donna enrolled in college as a communications major, and for the first six weeks of the semester, kept it her secret. When she finally revealed her secret to her family, they were dumbfounded, but since it had not interfered with their lives, they only snickered as they wished her "good luck." Between dropping kids off in the morning, chauffeuring them to their extra-curricular activities in the afternoon, keeping the house running smoothly, and preparing dinner everyday, it took Donna six years to complete her degree. By the time she graduated, Donna's family had become her greatest fans. Her graduation day was the proudest day of her life. (She was the oldest student in her class.)

Having had a taste of self discovery and her innate potential, there was no stopping Donna now. When she again shared her desire to pursue her calling, she was greeted with the same unsupportive comments from her family. Knowing she had to keep her momentum up, or get swallowed back into being a slave to others and estranged from herself, Donna once again secretly enrolled, this time in an eight-month course to become a licensed financial planner and life insurance agent. Having successfully circumnavigated the momentum malfunctions presented by her family, Donna's confidence began to soar. "Even-though I still had no idea where all of this was leading, I knew, for the first time, I was on track and heading toward something very important to me."

Donna received her license and was ready to venture into the "world of adults." Short-term jobs selling at a department store and designing closets were followed by several months researching various entrepreneurial opportunities. Throughout all of this, her husband's desire to keep here at home threatened, as it had so many years before, to bring her crashing back to earth. Though she still felt ill prepared to support herself, Donna knew that to achieve escape velocity, she had to remain focused on her intention. She knew she couldn't afford to continue fighting daily for her need to grow. Scared, but committed, Donna gathered her nerve and asked for a "trial separation." Though she had no idea how she would ever support herself, she was grateful when her husband agreed to the separation and financial support. Donna believed this was temporary and was overjoyed to learn to fly with the net her husband's support represented.

Donna found a $15 per hour job as an assistant to one of the partners of a well-established ad agency. Several months into her new job, Donna and I began to work together. Though she loved her job and enjoyed being really good at what she did, she was genuinely concerned how this job could ever become an adequate livelihood. I assured her it appeared tailor-made for her and suggested, as an experiment, she volunteer for every assignment that came through the door for the next three months. I explained that employers at small companies love people that can successfully wear lots of different hats. Within a month of beginning her experiment, two employees were laid off and a majority of their responsibilities were shifted to Donna's able shoulders. In no time at all, Donna's can-do attitude had made her a valued and indispensable member of the firm. Her employers praise was followed by her first raise, but the real boost to her confidence kicked in when she was asked to interview and write bios for the company's newest client; a firm specializing in financial planning. Donna's personal training as a financial planner enabled her to ask the perfect questions and to formulate a niche strategy that uniquely distinguished them in the marketplace. Donna's stock went through the ceiling when the clients signed a two-year contract and expressed how impressed they

> *If people knew how hard I worked to get my mastery, it wouldn't seem so wonderful at all.*
>
> Michelangelo

were with how she portrayed and positioned them. Again, in the mysterious way that so often occurs, Donna's experience as an insurance agent made her next assignment, writing copy for a life insurance company, a slam dunk.

After only a couple of months on the job, Donna received her second raise and the title of her choosing. When we last talked, Donna spoke of being overjoyed to be earning her living, doing what she loves, for people who value and appreciate her. She still thinks it's amazing she was guided to a place where her skills, gifts, and interests are her job description and where she is continuously offered opportunities to grow in directions she never even dared to dream were possible. "So do you think you've found your calling," I asked. Her face lit up, "Everyday a little more … but, if I'm not, I'm definitely on course."

Prodigy Practice #31 – Momentum Malfunctions: What's Holding You Back?

- The Power of Sacrifice

Prodigies are willing to make sacrifices because nothing matters more than developing their gift. Historically, sacrifice is perceived as having to give up something you want, for something you need. For example, as teenagers we were told that "if you want to go to college you had better do your homework, be home by ten and buckle down. There'll be time for fun later." Many of us were asked to give up what we wanted in the now, for some intangible future. As we grow older, we continue sacrificing what we want and love (in the here and now), to earn a living, be responsible, and put money away for retirement. One of the problems with this kind of thinking is when you give up the now, you often end up giving up many of the things you're passionate about, your connection to your inner prodigy and the likelihood that you'll ever stumble upon your calling. Over time you eventually come to realize that when you put your life and your loves off until tomorrow, Tomorrow Never Comes. It's no wonder with so many people adopting this life style that sacrifice has gained such a bad rap.

When it comes to people pursuing their calling, sacrifice has a completely different meaning. They don't give up what they love; they give up what gets in the way of doing what they love. They don't give up what they want for what they think they need; they give up what gets in the way of achieving their dreams. They sacrifice spending an excess of time and energy with the people, situations, and distractions that interfere with and impede their progress. They sacrifice illusions like, "I don't have enough time to work on my dream," "I don't have enough money," "There's no way," "But what about my family and kids?" "Nothing will ever come of it anyway." Instead of generating excuses and being the victim of their responsibilities, they use every free moment, become super inventive, and do whatever it takes, even if it's minimal, to engage in their passion. The kinds of sacrifices prodigies make are like cutting loose the sandbags from a hot air balloon so that it will ascend. When you cut loose—sacrifice—those things that are holding you back, you can't help but take off.

A powerful tool for taking the sting out of sacrifices is to practice re-framing. Re-framing allows you to take a situation you might otherwise experience as difficult or distasteful and transform it into a potential source of pleasure, a would-be win and long-term gift by looking at it in the light of what you will get out of the situation. It's most easily understood in the statement, "If I give this up—then I get to do this." Reframing can be illustrated by the difference in approaches to dieting and weight loss. When we've framed dieting in the negative it often shows up as, "I'm on a diet, and I can't eat any of the foods I love if I want to lose weight." Not only is this a poor way to assure success and an excellent way to assure failure and unhappiness, but also at its root, it denies the very reasons we probably chose to change our eating habits—we're unhappy with our current self-image; we have a poor health prognosis; or we're unable to participate in life because we are over-weight. When you re-frame your sacrifice, it will probably include the positive benefits that will result from your diet. "If I give up sugar, bread and late night binging, I'll be slim and feel good about that bikini vacation in the Bahamas; I'll be able to play with my grandchildren at the beach and take them for hikes in nature; My husband and I will start dancing and having sex like rabbits again; I'll enjoy good health, being able to breath freely and do whatever I please; I'll be eating foods that make me feel good about myself while I eat them."

> *Every act of creation is first of all an act of destruction.*
>
> Picasso

Remember, not every sacrifice requires going cold turkey. Some sacrifices only require that you change the way you think about what you're doing and how you react to it, which in turn changes your relationship to it from undermining to supportive. For example, you have a friend you really love but every time you get together "to chat" it ends up in a marathon that eats up your day or stretches too late into the night. You end up coming away from these "love fests" feeling exhausted, resentful or deflated. You could re-frame this relationship by saying; 1) "I absolutely love being with so and so for one or two hours." 2) "Being with so and so is like eating a really good meal. If I eat until I'm full, I feel deeply nourished and satisfied, if I over eat I feel sick, sluggish and resentful." If you can re-frame this relationship with an eye to fulfilling your calling, you will know exactly when enough is enough and walk away from your time together feeling the love, support and pleasure of your friend's company.

As your desire to embody your calling grows, sacrifices on behalf of your prodigy's intentions will become crystal clear, a whole lot easier, and a source of pleasure rather than a cause of pain or regret. As you practice the Power of Sacrifice you will naturally begin to re-frame all the aspects of your life that interfere with the Quest to discover your calling. In addition, distractions, addictions and antiquated beliefs will begin to dissolve and eventually disappear.

> *Your talents indicate and, to a degree, limit what you can do. Your expectations determine what you will do.*
>
> "*How to Find the Work You Love*"
>
> Laurence G. Boldt

Prodigy Story:

Ingmar Bergman, the famous filmmaker, musing as an adult, recalled the tremendous impact of his first trip to the cinema. Walking home from the theater he spoke of being, "overcome with a fever that has never left me." He'd been exposed to photographs previously but it wasn't until he saw moving pictures that everything shifted for him. Sometime, soon after his visit to the cinema, his parents committed what he experienced as the ultimate betrayal; they gave his brother a cinematograph (a primitive motion picture projector) for Christmas. Young Ingmar wailed for hours. After falling asleep with a broken heart, Ingmar awoke later that same night committed to, what for him was an enormous sacrifice; he offered his brother his prized collection of 100 tin soldiers. Though the price was high there was nothing he would let stand between him and what he was yet to know as his calling. The next morning, cinematograph in his possession, Ingmar set the projector up in a large closet he could make totally dark and private by closing the door. He then tells how he "lit the paraffin lamp and directed the beam of light … . A picture of a meadow appeared … asleep in the meadow was a young woman. Then I turned the handle! It is impossible to describe this. But at any time, I can recall the smell of the hot metal, the scent of mothballs and dust in the wardrobe, the feel of the crank against my hand … the trembling rectangle on the wall. I turned the handle and the girl woke up, slowly got up, stretched her arms out … . She was moving." The simple, yet enormous sacrifice of young Ingmar opened the door to his discovering his calling and to a lifetime of joy that benefited millions. (Bibliography: Cradles of Eminence)

Prodigy Practice #32 – Re-Framing: Re-frame your sacrifices as accelerators.

- Critical Path

The concept of critical path was born when scientists disproved the collective wisdom that the shortest distance between two points is a straight line. There are an infinite number of variables, known and unknown, that influence our journey and make traveling in a straight line virtually impossible. For example, if you were driving from the U.S. to the tip of South America, it might be faster, safer, and require less energy to go an extra 1,000 miles "out of your way" to avoid the rising Amazon or a country at war.

Scientists have determined that a spacecraft traveling between the earth and some distant target in space loosely inscribes a large, sweeping, imperfect arc, and is actually on course for a very small percentage of the time. They don't worry about this, instead they determine when the craft is beginning to deviate too far off course (this is determined as the point at which it has lost too much of its forward motion), calculate a course correction, fire the engines for an instant (to course correct) and resume their journey with relative ease.

To master navigating Critical Path:

1. Pay attention to where you're going,
2. Hold the reins loosely
3. Stay alert so that you recognize as you begin to drift off course
4. Seek the guidance of your support system, mentors, and intuition.
5. Course correct as often as needed
6. Revise your itinerary, chart a new course or define a new goal if needed.

By consciously engaging the dynamic process of navigating critical path, you set the stage to consciously participate in the magical interplay between your prodigy within (its vision of your calling), benevolent intent and the ever-shifting needs and demands of the world at large.

In our passion to discover our calling, it's easy to push ahead blindly, believing that our desire and drive will carry us directly to our envisioned goal. Since so much of the process of discovering our calling is dependent on perfecting communication with the prodigy, paying attention to benevolent intent and developing a tolerance for ambiguity, it is highly unlikely that where you assume you are going has any more than a passing resemblance to where you will actually end up. When you're willing to embrace the concept of critical path and thereby the necessity of course correction, you create an insurance policy that pays off in spades when you run head-on into an unpredictable detour, synchronistic opportunity, or new information that requires you to reassess your goals and beliefs. If, on the other hand, you decide to clutch tightly to your plan, disregard the voice of benevolent intent and blindly charge forward, it's likely you'll experience confusion, disorientation and setbacks. It's this kind of tunnel vision that often times results in disillusion, delusion, and self-abandonment.

> *If you don't know where you're going you'll probably end up somewhere else.*
>
> Yogi Bera

For many years, I ran 5 to 15 miles every day on mountain trails. With my lungs burning and heart pounding, I'd leap over boulders, cross streams, scramble up gravel slides and stumble down steep inclines, all the while attempting to navigate my way to a distant peak. Needless to say, I learned a lot about critical path and course correction. I learned how to successfully navigate any challenging undertaking: you must pay attention to what's right in front of you, what's coming up soon, and where you are ultimately aiming to be.

The 3 Levels of Course Correction:

Level 1: Beneath My Feet

Beneath My Feet course correction is where you're watching every step. Is there gravel, debris, or exposed roots? Is the ground uneven? Is the surface loose, does it change every few feet? Do I need to give it most of my attention or only peripheral awareness? In Level 1, you're constantly assessing: what's next, next, next? On rugged terrain and dangerous ascents, Level I will require the greatest degree of focus, awareness and adjustments. On well-traveled roads, it will probably require the least attention, only an occasional glance "beneath my feet."

Level 2: The Road Ahead

As a runner, The Road Ahead was about focusing on the area from ten feet in front of me to several hundred feet. It's not the details, and it's not the ultimate goal; it's the mid-range. It includes planning, adjusting, considering, watching for forks in the road, detours and quagmires. This is where most of life and most course corrections take place. On more than one occasion, as I raced along a trail, I became too focused on my feet and the result was often disastrous. I ran right trails, rolled down near vertical cliffs, stumbled over sagebrush or splashed face first into streams.

> *Start where you are, with what you have, knowing that what you have is plenty enough.*
>
> Booker T. Washington

Level 3: The Ultimate Goal

As a mountain runner, the Ultimate Goal was the distant peak. The deal with the distant peak is you can't just set your sights on it and head straight there. Talk about critical path: you may have to go up one ridge down into a canyon, across a stream, traverse fifteen switchbacks, scramble up a rock slide, drop down into another canyon, go half way around the back side and then scale the face. When you're looking at the distant peak, you know where you're going, but that doesn't mean you have any idea how you are actually going to get there. Whether you're attacking the summit, heading for the moon or intuiting your way toward your calling, you can be sure of one thing: it will not go exactly as planned. The best plan is to embrace the adage "the only constant is change." On your way to the Ultimate Goal the expectation of change will keep you awake, aware, and responsive to whatever arises.

So here's the way the 3 Levels of Course Correction pertain to discovering your calling:

1. You must be aware of all 3 Levels at all times.

2. You must be able to fluidly shift your focus from what's directly in front of you to what's coming up in the near future, and from there to your Ultimate Goal.

3. You must become proficient at integrating this information (preferably in real time), adjusting your calculations and making the necessary course corrections as gracefully and effortlessly as possible.

Our ability to receive guidance from our prodigy for the express purpose of navigating critical path is akin to an astronaut's relationship to Mission Control. The prodigy is not paralyzed or deceived by the necessity to course correct, it is in fact a very essential part of its job. When we remain dialed in to the frequency of the prodigy within, our Quest is under the masterful guidance of Mission Control. When the prodigy is in charge of navigating our critical path, a deep feeling of acceptance, relaxation and timeliness pervades our Sense of Divine Urgency.

Prodigy Story:

Alexandra had long cherished her dream of being a triple threat in the world of entertainment—singer/songwriter, actress, and writer/producer. For ten years she worked in an endless succession of restaurants as either a waitress, cook or bartender. She spent her free time writing songs and screenplays; practicing guitar and piano; and trying to get meetings with agents, record producers, and studio executives. Though Alexandra was talented, driven, and focused, none of the plans she made or projects she developed ever quite made it to fruition. Every time she'd get close to being signed by a record label, land a role or sell a script, the rug would be pulled out from under her. What always astounded me was, even-though she would stumble or crash, she always had the wisdom to go on retreat or take a short vacation to make contact with Mission Control. During these periods, she'd re-determine her critical path by assessing her options. She'd make the necessary course corrections by shifting her focus or resurrecting one of her other projects, and then she'd jump back in with fierce passion and renewed inspiration. The real testimony to Alexandra's commitment to her Quest was that, without any major victories to fuel her, she always managed to renew her Sense of Divine Urgency. At her darkest moments, she returned to her long-term goals to determine true north, called on her intuition to clarify the road ahead, and trusted her feelings (prodigy) to keep her from stumbling into the abyss.

> *I learned this, at least, by my experiment; that if one advances confidently in the direction of his dreams, and endeavors to live the life which he has imagined, he will meet with a success unexpected . . . .*
>
> Henry David Thoreau

At one point, after yet another dream fizzled in the eleventh hour, Alexandra was offered an opportunity to teach music at a private school near where she lived. In spite of her belief that it was "just temporary," one school led to another and Alexandra suddenly found herself with a number of schools, several employees, and a thriving business. Though she was no longer working as a triple threat in the restaurant business (waitress, bartender, cook), she still constantly questioned whether she'd betrayed her dreams. Instead of spending her free time working on projects that never saw the light of day, her time was consumed managing her music school. Though it wasn't her dream, she became wildly successful. What was even more important, her work became a continuous source of validation, acknowledgment, and though she hated to admit it, extraordinary joy.

After one year of rapid expansion accompanied by the ongoing feeling that she'd sold her dreams out, Alexandra began entertaining offers to sell the business. Though she wouldn't receive a lot of money from the sale, she rationalized the money would buy her the time and freedom she needed to recommit to her purpose. That was until the universe threw her a curve ball. In the middle of the negotiations to sell the business, the dean of one of the private schools where she taught approached her with an offer that would ultimately fold all of her gifts, talents, and dreams into her business. The dean told her how he had been leaned on by several of the most influential parents, who also happened to be the largest financial contributors, to present two stage shows a year—one prior to Christmas vacation and the other before summer break. When Alexandra responded with stunned silence, the principal sheepishly told her he didn't know who to turn to and wondered if she had any experience with "staging this kind of show." As Alexandra sat silent considering the possibilities, the principal expressed his exasperation with the "meddling mothers" when he added, "Oh yes, they would prefer the shows to be musicals."

Alexandra was dumbfounded that all of her years of pursuing her goal, charting her critical path, and laying out her endless course corrections had never led her to consider this as a possibility. She temporarily abandoned her plans to sell the business and jumped into writing, producing, and directing. The first year she produced two well-known musicals that were well received. The following year, in addition to producing and directing, she created the entire show—including writing the songs, music, and story. They were a smash. Word got out and the following year the other schools her company serviced requested she work her magic for them as well. Alexandra now produces audio and video recordings of the shows and distributes a growing line of books, tapes, and DVDs.

> *Our age has a particular mission … the creation of a civilization founded upon the spiritual nature of work.*
>
> Simon Weil

Though Alexandra always knew her ultimate goal and continuously charted her critical path, she only thought she knew how she'd get there. What finally took her beyond how she imagined it might happen was her ability to go with the flow, practice course correction and adapt to benevolent intent as it manifested in her life. Ultimately Alexandra's critical path led her past her wildest dreams and directly into her life's purpose.

Prodigy Practice #33 – Course Correction: Perfect the 3 levels of course correction.

- Immunized by the Gods

As we experience ourselves living on purpose and living a life of service, we come to acknowledge our expanding position as co-creators. When this happens, the way we live, learn and grow goes through a subtle yet radical transformation. Our consciousness shifts from survival and lacking to grace and gratitude. Prior to living on purpose, life is ruled by survival consciousness: "There's not enough to go around; I've got to fight for everything I need; I've got to figure out everything that could possibly go wrong so that I never have to experience lack or pain again."

Oftentimes, when our motivation is rooted in survival consciousness, even our successes are accompanied by a feeling of spiritual and emotional emptiness. As more and more people undertake the quest to discover their calling, an entire generation stands poised to make the quantum leap from survival to grace. This leap has already arrived as a shift in consciousness and priorities and will continue to gain momentum as each of us:

1. Discovers our gift
2. Aligns with our Archetypes of Service
3. Accepts direction from the prodigy within
4. Accepts the guidance that shows up in our lives as a manifestation of benevolent intent
5. Takes actions motivated by what is the highest and best for all concerned.

By committing to developing your gift, being of service, and taking appropriate action, you become immunized by the prodigy to the patterns, fears, and doubts that have undermined you in the past. In other words, as you begin to embody your calling, you become protected from many of the distractions, detours, and pitfalls that previously destroyed your momentum and derailed your intentions. As you enjoy a heightened sense of contact with your core purpose, a sense of divine urgency accompanies the feeling of being the right person in the right place, at the right time, making the right contribution.

Prodigy Story:

As Evan tells it, "I was down on my luck, just getting by, giving tennis lessons to the children of the well-heeled. I'd recently failed at becoming a movie director, owed a ton of money, felt stuck, and had no idea where I was going. I knew I had a passion for design, but because I had no training or degree, I had given up on it as well. The only joy I was experiencing was playing around designing things on the computer. I tried everything I could think of to climb out of the hole I was in but neither prayer nor my best thinking were good enough to get me out of it."

> *Success on any major scale requires you to accept responsibility . In the final analysis, the one quality that all successful people have... is the ability to take on responsibility.*
>
> Michael Korda

When Evan and I first began talking, it was clear he was frustrated and upset by his situation. I suggested, as a way to shake up the void he was experiencing, that he offer everyone he knew his design services for free. Though Evan couldn't see how this would ever amount to a living, let alone his calling, he figured that since he had nothing else to do, it would kill time until he found his way back into the movie business. With some trepidation, Evan began getting the word out that he was willing to help anyone and everyone with their design jobs. Soon, his portfolio of "freebies" built an impressive resume. Shortly thereafter, he received his first paying gig and from there on, one job led to the next. Through working continuously Evan honed his talent, ignited his passion to learn more, and opened the door to greater and greater opportunities.

Evan's steady stream of work placed him directly in the path of continuous positive feedback regarding his talent, which began to immunize him to his old self-destructive and deprecating tendencies. His self-esteem soared as he recognized the positive influence his gift was having in the lives of friends and clients. He began taking classes, committed to learning a new piece of software with every job, and began to entertain the idea that maybe he had discovered, if not his calling, then at least the path to it.

After several months of being the beneficiary of benevolent intent, arriving "out of nowhere" as a steady stream of opportunities, Evan was offered a full-time job doing computer graphics at a film company that specialized in movie trailers. In the past, a break of this magnitude would have generated a slew of paralyzing feelings of not being good enough or being "an impostor." Instead, Evan, immunized by his prodigious accomplishments, graciously accepted the job with little of his old self-doubt. Within months of being hired, Evans design work took a quantum leap. His employers offered him the chance to re-ignite his passion for filmmaking by expanding his responsibilities to include editing trailers and directing the company's first short film. "Who would've known that doing pro bono computer design work would have led me back to my real love?"

Evan recently told me though the old feelings of fear and doubt have not totally disappeared, they "no longer star in the leading role." Instead, he experiences a feeling of confidence when new opportunities are presented—a confidence that comes from being valued for his contributions. He now knows that everyday more of his life's purpose is being revealed to him and his "Higher Power" (the prodigy within) never gives him more than he can handle.

Prodigy Practice #34 – Survival to Grace: Assess your posture toward your calling.

CHAPTER 9

Principle #7:

EXERCISE THE WILLINGNESS TO SUCCEED

The willingness to succeed is not just the will to succeed. The will to succeed is the commitment, passion, and drive that come with expecting the best. The willingness to succeed is the ability to embrace success when—and as—it arises, not to resist it, deny it or undermine it. When we acknowledge that benevolent intent has guided our personal journey and the prodigy within has played a key role in many of the important decisions in our life, our shadow begins to unravel and transform into our ally. When this happens, our ability to embrace success begins to outweigh the negative programming we may have internalized. Over time, as we continue to open to the realm of infinite possibilities, our willingness to succeed continues to grow exponentially.

Of all of the 7 Principles of Prodigy, the willingness to succeed is perhaps the most elusive and confusing. If you were raised to believe that nothing you ever did was quite good enough, then your willingness to succeed was most likely affected. If you have had successes that nonetheless often ended in some form of failure, then you probably want to consider how willing you actually are to succeed. A lack of willingness to succeed can take many forms: you transform your company, increasing revenue twofold, only to be fired for not sharing the political views of the board of directors; you're successful at introducing a revolutionary new product and then suffer a devastating lawsuit; you and your spouse work obsessively to attain your mutual goals only to end up divorced because you've grown apart.

> *I failed over and over and over again in my life. And that is why I succeed.*
>
> Michael Jordan

No matter how your willingness to succeed has been compromised, it is essential that you identify it and then work to regenerate it if you are truly committed to succeeding in your quest to discover and live your calling.

• Fear of Failure, Fear of Success

Until we become aware of the demoralizing effect of our fear of failure and fear of success, we will never be ready to embrace and embody our willingness to succeed. It's not that prodigies don't fear success and failure—frequently they do even more so than the rest of us—it's that they do not buckle under, give up or abandon their calling in the face of those fears. Either through sheer tenacity, the unbearable feeling that they dare not betray their destiny, or the total denial of their fears, prodigies keep on track, even as the guillotine of fear slices to the bone.

For most of us, fear of failure and fear of success are inextricably interwoven. So often you hear people comment on their fear of failure when, in fact, if they were to look deeper, they might discover that what they fear even more is success. If, as a child, you are taught what you do is "not good enough" or your best efforts are going to fall short of others' expectations, it would seem perfectly natural that you would become afraid of failing. But when you fall short of your parents' or teachers' expectations, you often get more attention than when you succeed. Even though this kind of attention is negative, it may be the only attention you get. When this scenario of negative attention plays out again and again in scholastic endeavors, team sports and personal interests, it's natural that one might become dependent on the attention and equate it with love. After continuously falling short of our parents' (and internalized parents') expectations, many of us have developed the tendency to turn the successes we do have into failures. Over time we become afraid of succeeding because the fear of an unknown experience far outweighs the attention and negative love you know you'll receive when you fail.

> *A man' errors are his portals of discovery*
>
> James Joyce

Once you identify your ability to pursue success and accept it when it arrives, you shift into a willingness to embrace your calling. When you know you use perfectionism to diminish your successes, dwell on your feelings of not having done it right; support your feelings of not being good enough, or reinforce your unworthiness because you have not been properly acknowledged—then you are ready to accept success in another guise. Until you take responsibility for the ways you sabotage your best efforts, you will always default to your original programming. On the other hand, as you continue to unravel the negative beliefs that make up your hard-wiring, your willingness to succeed will rise effortlessly.

So how do you go about transforming your fears of success and failure into the joyous experience of manifesting your calling? First, you become willing to recognize when your fears of success or failure are having a negative effect on you. Next, you learn to identify the triggering mechanisms, the thoughts and events that generate the feelings that send you into a tailspin. When you've recognized these fears and their respective triggering mechanisms, you are in a position to identify what it is you are really afraid of. It might be the acknowledgment that comes with success, or maybe it's being held accountable for your actions, or fear of commitment or fear of rejection. Armed with the recognition of how your fear of success or failure manifests, you are prepared to understand and assess the price you've paid for being the victim of these feelings. It is important to note that the paralysis that accompanies these fears always results in falling short of our dreams, our goals and, above all, our life's purpose. Finally, you choose to turn to the prodigy to distinguish between realistic concerns and historical ones and to receive the guidance and support you require to take decisive action in the face of whatever fears may persist.

Everything comes to him who hustles while he waits.

Thomas A. Edison

Prodigy Story:

Throughout his life Zeke had allowed his father to "guide" him in all of his major decisions, personal and professional. As a boy, Zeke wanted to play soccer, but his father's dream of his son being a baseball star won out. As he grew older and wanted to be an interior decorator, his father's words once again prevailed upon him, "That's no kind of a job for a man. Besides, no matter what you do in life you can always use a business degree." Zeke had become so afraid of failing at what he was passionate about he became willing to trade his passions for mediocrity to win his father's love and respect.

After graduating with a degree in business, Zeke rolled right into a high paying position as a market research analyst. With his degree, executive title, and father's otherwise guarded praise, Zeke enjoyed a level of self-respect and self-esteem he had never before experienced. He loved the fun and challenge of his job, but above all he relished the fruits of his labor and the support and admiration he received from his father.

The job became tedious and redundant over the next 15 years. His father's support slowly faded as Zeke failed to scale the heights his father deemed appropriate to his son's potential. Zeke felt trapped, devalued and afraid to do anything else; after all, it was the only job he'd ever had as a grown-up. When he was really honest with himself, he didn't know if he was more afraid of continuing to succeed at something he hated or of taking the chance of failing at something he was passionate about.

As so often happens when we sell ourselves out, something else must give. In this case, it was Zeke's mental health. It started with insomnia, and escalated into low-grade anxiety. Finally he was diagnosed with major depressive disorder. Zeke had found his way out by failing to be a success in his own mind and heart. Over the next couple of years, Zeke spent a small fortune on therapy and antidepressants while his father made it his personal mission never to let him forget he was a quitter and a disappointment. The only joy Zeke experienced during this period was when he practiced yoga, decorated his condo, or helped his friends painting, designing, and refurbishing their houses.

As his savings began to dwindle and he started dipping into his 401k, Zeke, out of desperation, took a $10/hour job at a plant and flower shop. The job, though demeaning in his eyes and proof positive of his loser status in his father's eyes, quickly became a bastion of mental health and a source of pride for Zeke. He found great pleasure in his weekly trips to clients' businesses and homes to tend their plants and renew their floral arrangements. Zeke's passion for design and love of people helped him increase the stores accounts by 25 percent in just a couple of months.

> *God respects me when I work, but he loves me when I sing.*
>
> Rabindrinath Tapore

After six months on the job, Zeke gathered his courage to request a raise and a "piece of the action" for the clients he had generated. When his employer dismissed his request and devalued his efforts, Zeke's feelings of failure arose with a vengeance. Then, to Zeke's surprise, one of the clients he'd brought to the shop offered to bankroll him in his own plant store and introduce him to the other businesses in the client's high-rise. As Zeke recalls, the unexpected generosity and encouragement of a near stranger was enough to tip the scales: "Something clicked and I just knew this was what I wanted to do and I would be successful at it."

One year later, Zeke is thriving. Not only is his plant and flower business growing but also a steady stream of design work has begun to show up. Though Zeke still occasionally experiences bouts of depression, they are no longer paralyzing, and are usually replaced by the joy he experiences from doing what he loves. An unforeseen miracle occurred recently when Zeke was at his parents' house for a party and overheard his father bragging to his golf buddies about how proud he was of his son's "amazing success." Neither paralyzed by a fear of success or failure, Zeke is now enjoying the ride of his life as his calling continues to reveal itself in new and unpredictable ways.

Prodigy Practice #35 – Fears, Triggers & Remedies: How do you abandon success?

- The Art of Receiving – Just Say Yes

The single most powerful thing you can do to generate a willingness to succeed is to exercise your ability to just say yes to what life has to offer. It's easy to assume when something you perceive as bad, problematic, or the result of some character flaw happens that it means you've screwed up, wandered off-course and must take immediate action to fix things. However, if you've made it this far, it's time to consciously and consistently believe that your prodigy within is involved in guiding you on your quest to discover your calling. When you know this to be true, it's much easier to recognize what the prodigy would have you do next.

Compliments, apparent misfortune, uninvited suggestions, strange job offers, the unexpected termination of a relationship—these are all opportunities to acknowledge that your prodigy is taking over the controls and requesting that you just say yes. Knowing the prodigy might be the motivating force behind a given situation begs that you pause, reflect and be open to seeing what good may be within a circumstance that is not immediately obvious. By choosing to remain open the muscle of intuition develops and you begin to practice the art of receiving. What have you got to lose? Remember, this chapter is called exercising a willingness to succeed—not having or knowing or being, but exercising. Saying yes does not mean you must accept every situation or that you cannot change your mind at any time, it only means that you'll look things over thoroughly and take them out for a test drive. When you are not sure what is being offered, allow extra time for the gift that might be just beneath the surface to be revealed. By learning to just say yes you empower the universe to support you in ways that are beyond your limited imagination or wildest expectations. You transform a trickling stream of guidance from the prodigy into a raging river of support and insight. You magnify your willingness to succeed.

Prodigy Story:

A client of mine, Jorge, who after years of frustration as a still-not-produced screenwriter accepted an offer that just wouldn't go away. A large corporation leader, to whom Jorge had pitched numerous ideas, made him an unexpected offer to head the company's new multi-million dollar division, whose sole purpose was to finance, produce and market films and projects to the exploding Latin American market. By just saying yes, all of Jorge's gifts and skills were mobilized in a powerful, meaningful, and uplifting way. Instead of struggling on his own, Jorge now works with writers and producers who wouldn't return his calls before. He is fulfilling his need to collaborate, instead of being the lone—and lonely—screenwriter. He is not only making use of the MBA he spent six years obtaining and six more years trying to forget, but he's become a positive force in the Latino community. Jorge's commitment to make a difference, help his community, express his creativity, and put his master's degree to use all come into play daily. By just saying yes to a situation that didn't fit his picture of how his life and work would manifest, Jorge ended up inheriting the life he'd always dreamt of.

Prodigy Practice #36 – Just Say Yes: Learn to practice the art of receiving.

- Starving the Dweller on the Threshold

The dweller on the threshold is the being that has formed around the internalized negativity of our past. The dweller materializes as the embodiment of all our failures, karma, habitual patterns of lack and limitation, doubt, harsh words (toward ourselves and others) and egocentric tendencies to personalize everything. In the world of metaphysics, the dweller is understood to be an entity whose sole purpose for existing is to keep us from realizing our full spiritual potential. Like a dragon that terrorizes the countryside, kidnaps the princess, and destroys every noble knight who sets forth to slay it, the dweller wreaks havoc in our souls. And like the dragons of mythology, the dweller uses the threat of fear, terror, and torture (on the physical, emotional, and mental planes) to keep us small, afraid, distracted, and disconnected from the prodigy within us.

> *We all wear marks, and the time comes when we cannot remove them without removing some of our skin.*
>
> Andre Berthiaume

The dweller on the threshold is conceived, born and raised on that which has found sanctuary in both our personal and collective unconscious. Your dweller may have been conceived and fed by:

1. A lifetime of half-hearted efforts.

2. All of the times you missed the mark and passed judgment on youself.

3. A parent or authority figure's demeaning and degrading comments about you.

4. A collection of your past feelings and experiences of failure.

5. Negative agreement realities: those ideologies and beliefs that reside unexamined in the collective unconscious which are widely held to be the truth, yet tend to undermine your belief in yourself and the wisdom of the prodigy within you. These negative agreement realities that feed the dweller can be 1) gender based: "Women are not good at sports" or "Men make the best CEOs"; 2) social in nature: "You can't make it in politics if you're not a WASP" or "People on welfare have no motivation"; 3) religious beliefs: "Anyone who does not believe in (my) God is doomed to eternal damnation"; 4) age specific: "If you're not young you can't make it in Hollywood" or "You can't compete with these kids that are fresh out of college"; 5) education based: "You must have the necessary degrees" or "No one will take you seriously without a Ph.D."

> *Human beings can alter their lives by altering their attitudes of mind.*
>
> William James

Ultimately the dweller, whether residing in our personal or collective unconscious, is like a ghost that haunts a house. Until it is exposed and exorcised, it will remain a constant intruder, a source of endless chaos and wholly committed to wreaking havoc on the intentions of the prodigy within. Just attempting to act in accordance with the promptings of the prodigy often awakens the dweller from its position, slumbering like a gargoyle, at the threshold of our calling. When awakened by positive actions, it unleashes a flood of unconscious destructive tendencies and a barrage of negative and undermining thought forms designed to fill our minds with doubt and our hearts with fear. The dweller sits on the threshold of our higher self, intent on reminding us that we will never amount to any more than who we've been and preventing us from ever becoming fully conscious of we really are. Its sole purpose is to destroy our willingness to succeed by continuously dissipating and undermining our best intentions.

Because the dweller is hard wired into the subconscious, eliminating its presence requires ferocious vigilance. You must learn to sense its approach, recognize its presence, and identify its voice. Each of our dwellers seductively and deviously employs specific phrases, enticements and images to distract and detour us from our calling. Once the dweller's negating, negative agenda has been identified, it can only be exorcised through starvation. There's an adage in spiritual circles often used to illuminate the process, "The only way to kill a mad dog is by starving it to death." So it is with the dweller. You must become conscious of its face, root out its food sources, and refuse to be seduced into supplying it the negative nutrients it requires to thrive. When you are no longer the dweller's slave, but instead standing guard, you will discover a new sense of strength, confidence and follow-through that will enhance your effort and determination to manifest your calling.

Prodigy Story:

Robert was inspired to become a doctor when he was eight years old by his favorite television series, *The Fugitive.* In the show, a doctor wrongly accused of murdering his wife, manages, at great risk to his own life, to do the right thing and continue to save others' lives. The idea a man could put his own life and freedom at risk to help others was inspiring to Robert in the way Superman was to his friends.

When Robert graduated from medical school and completed his residency, he thought working in ERs would be the best way to get a wide range of experience, help everyday people, save money, and steer his career towards the practice of holistic medicine.

That was the story he told himself.

Then there was the story his dweller continuously bombarded him with. In this story, he would only have to see patients once, he could remain half-hearted in his commitment, and he would never have to face the fact he was scared that maybe he couldn't really help people anyway. Even after 25 years at numerous ERs, Robert still voiced his dweller's opinion of his calling by referring to himself as a "hack mechanic." Every time he even began to contemplate a change, the voice of his dweller chanted a most compelling mantra of negativity: "Nothing's ever going to happen, ever going to change, it's always going to be the same."

> *Shame is the leading cause of death of actualizing one's giftedness.*
>
> Mary-Elaine Jacobson

Robert, like so many of us, had no problem finding people to give voice to the dweller: his mother, his ER director, and his supposed mentor. Each of these people voiced the negativity of his own dweller on the threshold, never missing opportunity to remind him that he was a failure, clumsy, self-centered without social skills and without them he was nothing.

Then one day it all snapped. Robert was ready to take a chance. He got into therapy, where he began to see the demoralizing influence of his mother and identify the prodigy-destructive tendencies of his dweller. Shortly thereafter he broke free of his mentor (his current externalized dweller), stepped out of the safety of ERs and accepted a job as medical director at an established holistic health clinic. Even with all the positive changes, it took Robert a long time, a great deal of patience, and a lot of positive support to leave behind the half-hearted person he had become. It took even longer for him to accept and forgive himself and step out from being victimized by his dweller on the threshold. As Robert began to live in alignment with his calling, the dweller's grip lessened. As a result of the passionate and whole-hearted commitment Robert was finally bringing to his work, he experienced a consistent feeling of hope and joy. In his newly resurrected state, Robert was free to receive the love, acceptance and gratitude of his friends, clients, and peers for the first time in his life.

> *Mars, Lord of Illusion, represents … all the unconscious elements within our psyche which fight against our liberation.*
>
> *"Buddha"*
>
> Karen Armstrong

Feeling a newfound confidence, Robert decided it was time to let his ER license expire. To his surprise that act momentarily reawakened the dweller: "You're going to end up destitute and in poverty. No one's going to want what you have to offer." But with the help of his friends and associates, Robert's prodigy within was ultimately victorious. In his ongoing commitment to deliver holistic health care to humanity, Robert now works at several clinics, speaks at conferences, and has written a book, *Healthy Medicine*, that addresses the diseased state of health care in America. In a recent conversation, Robert spoke of the extraordinary leap in his quality of life since wrestling it back from the dweller on the threshold. When he finished enumerating all of the positive things that were happening, he paused for a long moment and, with a distant look on his face, mused, "I look back on the life I'd settled for and wonder how I lived in the desert for so long."

Prodigy Practice #37 – Facing the Dweller: Learn to identify your dweller.

- Building a Hierarchy of Needs

One of the primary ways to exercise a willingness to succeed is to become intimately aware of your prodigy's hierarchy of needs. When you're hazy or lazy regarding your prodigy's requirements, it's easy to find yourself devaluing or sacrificing the very things critical to embodying your calling. By now you've probably gleaned a fairly clear picture of your prodigy's needs. You've probably also gained a practical, day-to-day, understanding of how you have ignored or devalued those needs in the past. Now that you are becoming aware of your prodigy's requirements, it's time to clarify their hierarchal relationship to one another. When you know the prodigy's hierarchy of needs you will effortlessly, economically, and intelligently stay the course. A true willingness to succeed is revealed when your personal needs and those of your prodigy become symbiotic and synergistic.

Just as each human being has a unique set of needs, and those needs have a precise hierarchical relationship to one another, so does each individual's prodigy within. Not only would it be impossible to come up with a one-size-fits-all set of needs that pertain to every prodigy, it would most likely be counterproductive and destructive. For example, one person's prodigy might have a hierarchy of needs that requires them to

1. Practice religiously
2. Avoid negative people
3. Eat breakfast

4. Accrue wins and build self-esteem
5. Generate momentum
6. Play hard.

Another person's prodigy (or the same person in another phase of life) may describe her hierarchy of needs in terms of her professional intentions: e.g., I intend to work

1. For a company improving the quality of life for the underprivileged
2. In a loving environment where I am acknowledged consistently
3. Where I sit at a desk fewer than two hours per day, am outdoors often and travel regularly
4. Where I have the entire summer off to travel
5. Where I can afford to tithe 10 percent of my income and save 15 percent.

If it is your intention to successfully live your calling, then it is of the utmost importance that you define your prodigy's hierarchy of needs. When the prodigy's needs are prioritized hierarchically, you will have a clear-cut means to assess what will support—and what will undermine—your prodigy on a moment-to-moment, decision-by-decision basis. Like a reference manual on self-respect, your hierarchy of needs can be used to guide, align, and direct your energies toward the realization of your gift.

For example, I discovered that, to show up for my prodigy while writing this book, I had to eat breakfast. As an adult, I've never been a breakfast eater. I've never liked it. I always felt mentally and physically sluggish after eating in the morning. Then one day I realized my writing was suffering because I expended so much energy early in the morning, (consulting, teaching and exercising) I was literally in starvation mode when I sat down to write around noon. As soon as I realized I was compromising my prodigy's primary need to write, breakfast moved up in my hierarchy of needs. Soon thereafter, benevolent intent handed me a recipe for a protein smoothie that is now an essential part of my morning regimen. By recognizing the critical relationship of eating breakfast to my clearly stated goal to write this book, it was easy to shift it up toward the top of my hierarchy of needs.

As you look to uncover your prodigy's hierarchy of needs, don't dismiss any requirement as too small, ridiculous, or impractical. Seemingly insignificant requests from your prodigy within like a daily plunge in the icy ocean, monthly visits to the museum, or a piece of chocolate broken into reward-size pieces and doled out throughout the day, can make the difference between success and failure. Any need that tweaks your fancy is a potentially important need, if only momentarily, and as such, deserves to be acknowledged, added to your hierarchy of needs and fulfilled when appropriate.

Prodigy Story:

After obtaining his MBA, Ted worked as a consultant while he tried to find his way into a job that was right for him. After a couple of frustrating months of not having his needs met, Ted decided to write out a "wish list" (hierarchy of needs). Ted's wish list included finding a job that 1) challenged him to use every one of his skills and talents; 2) would support him in growing into his true self; 3) would have him working with and for kind, supportive, and inspiring people; 4) would pay well, with large financial incentives and no ceiling on his income; and 5) would place him in service to his fellow humans. Ted felt, though there was some room for give and take, each of his needs would have to be fulfilled to some degree, or it would be a deal-breaker.

Armed with his wish list Ted went from one job interview to another, from one consulting gig to the next. After each interview, each consulting job, he'd go home and refer to his wish list, rating each opportunity from one to ten in terms of the likelihood that his needs and intentions would be fulfilled. If Ted had the slightest inkling one of the items on his wish list might not be satisfied, he'd return and question the interviewer, potential boss or other employees to gain the clarity he required to make an informed decision and thereby avoid wasting his precious time and energy. Through this process of using his hierarchy of needs as his map, Ted learned to trust his intuition by identifying the blind spots that had seduced him into making poor decisions in the past. After kissing a number of frogs, Ted was offered a job that seemed like "a perfect fit."

> *When you are inspired by some great purpose, some extraordinary project, all your thoughts break their bounds: Your mind transcends limitations, your consciousness expands in every direction, and you find yourself in a new, great and wonderful world. Dormant forces, faculties and talents become alive, and you discover yourself to be a greater person by far than you ever dreamed yourself to be.*
>
> Patanjali

The job, with a large company, entailed managing a new division, training a work force and moving out of state for two years. The pay, though not quite up to Ted's bottom line, would meet his requirements because his living expenses would be covered for the length of the contract. The long-term benefits looked great, and Ted was satisfied that the company and his co-workers were highly ethical and conscientious. In terms of Ted's hierarchy of needs, what made the job particularly attractive was he would be responsible for training an emerging work force in a depressed area, thereby making a direct contribution to other people's quality of life.

Ted, ecstatic at what he believed to be a perfect fit, began a six-month training regime. After a couple of months, Ted was enjoying his new job, but experiencing an inexplicable sense of agitation. He constantly questioned his feeling of agitation, wondering if maybe he was afraid of the enormous responsibility that went with the job, afraid of being away from home for so long, or of being discovered as a fraud. With the help of his mentor and friends, Ted resolved some of the issues he thought might be responsible, and yet the feeling that "something just wasn't right" continued to plague him.

> *I learned this, at least, by my experiments; that if one advances confidently in the direction of his dreams, and endeavors to live the life which he has imagined, he will meet with a success unexpected..*
>
> *Henry David Thoreau*

Frustrated and unwilling to disregard his emotions, Ted decided to visit a therapist he had worked with years before. Ted shared his wish list, talked in depth about how much he was enjoying the challenge, and spoke in glowing terms regarding what a positive experience the preparation was. Together they addressed the old fears and patterns they had explored earlier to see if they were playing a more significant roll than Ted was aware of. After several sessions of in-depth exploration, they agreed that, though these issues were present, they were not playing much of a role in his current situation.

On his fourth visit, Ted's therapist suggested they look at whether there was something that belonged on Ted's wish list he had overlooked or dismissed as unimportant. Immediately a light bulb went off for Ted. He knew instantaneously and with absolute certainty the source of his anxiety: he would be moving away from his 12-year-old son and aging parents. Even though Ted had gone to great lengths to make the situation work by sub-letting an apartment for weekend visits back home, researching airline and train schedules for travel between the two cities, obtaining his parents' blessing and getting his son excited about having two houses and "a lot of cool new things to do," Ted hadn't been aware of how he really felt about it. As soon as Ted clarified his needs, he knew that being near his family belonged at the top of his wish list.

Almost immediately following this realization, however, Ted felt a terrible sense of shame that he had somehow overlooked his family's importance in his life. Ted's therapist reminded him that he had acted respectfully and inclusively under the circumstances, considering when he wrote his wish list, the thought of relocating had never entered his mind as an option. Now that Ted was aware of his family's place in his hierarchy of needs, he knew with absolute certainty that moving away was a deal-breaker and even though he might never find another "perfect job," he would have to turn this one down.

When Ted and I first spoke he was feeling depressed and hopeless about having turned down "the opportunity of a lifetime." I shared with Ted my experience regarding my "opportunity of a lifetime" (the job I'd been offered in Singapore: see Prodigy Story - To Thine Own Prodigy Be True). I suggested perhaps something better was on the way. Though doubting he would ever find anything as good, Ted amended his wish list to include his family and some other needs he uncovered after doing several Prodigy Practices. Though he was out of his comfort zone, he did feel better knowing what he wanted and needed and was committed to try and make it happen. To Ted's utter amazement the opportunity of a lifetime arrived within weeks.

Ted's new job included all of the items on his amended wish list, fulfilled his prodigy's hierarchy of needs and even further clarified, in his mind, his true calling. Two months into his new career, Ted already refers to it as "the most exhilarating and fulfilling experience of my life."

Prodigy Practice #38 – Hierarchy of Needs: Generate a list of your prodigy's needs.

- Embodying the Prodigy Within

"I am what I am and that's all that I am, I'm Popeye the Sailor Man." Talk about embodying the prodigy within! Popeye's famous mantra of self-knowledge has inspired millions. Knowing who you are why you're here—and accepting it as more than enough, rather than pining to be more or different from who you actually are—is an extraordinary blessing and relief. As the Seven Principles of Prodigy become the motivation and guiding light behind more and more of your actions, you become the living expression of who you are meant to be: no longer defined by success or failure; no longer controlled by your past or bound to a limiting idea of your capabilities. You are finally free to show up for your calling, just as you intended. You are embodying the gift you alone have to give.

As you embody the prodigy within, you become a center of gravity—a powerful and attractive force in the world. Others perceive that you have something special to offer—presence, charisma. You've arrived at the place where you now draw the necessary people, circumstances, and resources around your visions. You serve as the causal center, assuming responsibility for the manifestation of the vision and intention your prodigy has inspired you to realize. Since you are now living your purpose, there will be times when you are not the center of an unfolding purpose, but find yourself attracted to another prodigy's intention. In this case, you arrive like a planet in someone else's solar system. You are still a center of gravity. You are an equal contributor. Your gift, your offering, and who you are, fit perfectly. You inhabit this role for as long or short as your prodigy within dictates. For some of us, offering our gift to another's purpose may be a lifelong practice, but because it is aligned with our greater purpose, it is the most effective way to be of service and in perfect integrity with our calling

> *In the final analysis we count for something only because of the essential we embody, and if we do not embody that, life is wasted.*
>
> C.G. Jung

Whenever individuals who are living their calling are drawn together to generate an intention, they form a cadre. A cadre is a group of individuals committed to offering their gift and vision to the realization of a collectively held intention. A cadre is bound together by its united calling and tends to organically coalesce for a specific purpose and then dissolve when the purpose has been realized. Members come and go as necessity and opportunity dictate. When someone leaves the group, the collectively held intention attracts another individual to fill the needed position. When we find ourselves a member of a cadre, we are not only embodying our prodigy's purpose; we are fulfilling a greater role, one that is far larger than the sum of its parts. Being a member of a cadre can, at different times, diminish our sense of separation from others, bring us an ever-deeper rapport with benevolent intent, and inspire us to recognize ourselves as co-creators with the one intelligence that guides us all.

Prodigy Story:

In Japan, there's a tradition of obtaining mastery (embodying the prodigy within) that dates back thousands of years. One of the arenas in which mastery has been raised to the highest form of art is the tea ceremony. In this rich and ancient custom, a tea master inducts people into a transcendental state through the contemplative dance of the tea ceremony.

There is a legend told of the most highly regarded tea master in Japan. One day, while sitting at an inn having a meal, the tea master watches as three drunken mercenaries began to harass the patrons. After several minutes the tea master called the mercenaries over to his table and suggested it would be best for everyone if they simply left. After the mercenaries finished laughing at the "silly old man," they upended his table, withdrew their swords, and demanded he defend himself. To protect the innocent people, the old man accepted their challenge and suggested they meet the following day at sunrise.

The tea master, knowing nothing of swordsmanship, went to Japan's greatest sword master, told him the story and requested he teach him to defend himself. At the least, he reasoned, he could die honorably. In reply, the swordsman requested the tea master perform the tea ceremony. The tea master replied that he did not have three hours to spare. The swordsman asked that he trust him and repeated his request. The tea master, though confused, knew better than to question the methods of a master, and prepared the tea ceremony. The swordsman quickly fell under the spell of the ceremony. He smiled as the tea master exhibiting the concentration of a master surgeon, the gracefulness of a master dancer, the precision of a master swordsman, and the perfect breath control of a meditation master, conducted the tea ceremony. When the tea master finished, he once again asked to be shown the way to defend his honor. This time the sword master acquiesced, enigmatically stating, "You will prepare for your duel just as you have served me tea."

He then proceeded to show the tea master the preparatory rituals of a master swordsman: the meditative approach to the field of battle, the impeccable attention to folding one's overcoat and the deep, ceremonial bow of respect for a worthy opponent. He then briefly instructed the tea master in the proper way to unsheathe the sword and assume the posture of a samurai ready for combat. The sword master then bowed respectfully. The tea master, feeling unprepared, requested to be shown how to wield the sword in battle. The sword master refused. "Your mastery is your only defense. I have taught you all that you will require to prevail."

> *If I am not for myself, who will be for me? If I am only for myself, what am I? If not now, when?*
>
> Ray Hillel

The next day at the appointed time, the tea master, with the same impeccable focus, precision and presence he had exhibited in the tea ceremony, approached the mercenaries. In an attempt to rile the "silly old man" they mocked him, made crude comments, and brandished their swords around his head. The tea master, with the concentration and intensity acquired from ten thousand tea ceremonies, proceeded through the precise choreography of a samurai master. The mercenaries grew quiet, then pensive, then finally disconcerted. Still, they thought, it was three against one. Then the tea master bowed with great reverence, reached for his sword with supernatural resolve, and unsheathed it in a large graceful sweeping arc. With his eyes fixed on eternity and his stance powerfully rooted in the now, the tea master's transformation was complete. In the overpowering presence of such mastery, the scales tipped and the mercenaries, convinced of their imminent demise, turned and fled.

The moral of the story is this: When we embody the prodigy

within, it glorifies every part of our lives, impacts everything we do and assures a level of success in any action we are guided to undertake.

Prodigy Practice #39 – Embodiment: Stating your arrival.

- Walking the Razor's Edge

Man's character is his genius

Heraclitus

Walking the razor's edge is about developing a commitment to discover your calling and demands that you remain fit, alert, and ready at all times. It requires you to learn to identify the precarious line between too much and too little, between what you send out and how it returns to you, between thinking you know where your life is going and remaining awed at how little control you actually have over it. By exercising your ability to walk the razor's edge you learn to see, feel and know what to do when things move off course. You gain the freedom to change quickly and acquire the presence of mind to do so accurately. You hone your ability to assess situations on the fly by recognizing the price of admission for engaging in them (the cost of indulging in a specific activity or relationship, measured in terms of time, energy and whether it supports or undermines your intention). You know, with a degree of certainty, what the Buddhist refers to as "right action." You stop generating paralyzing personal and emotional dramas and master the ability to move gracefully through life with open eyes, open hands, an open mind, and above all, an open heart. When walking the razor's edge, you are traveling the path of least resistance.

Prodigy Story:

Diana is a psychotherapist who serves as the director of counseling at A Place Called Home, an at-risk youth center that provides rehabilitation and intervention for former and potential gang members. In addition to her work as a psychotherapist, Diana is on the board of directors for the John Wayne Cancer Institute, has funded a colon cancer research program in her mother's name, and spearheaded the creation of a state-of-the-art speech pathology classroom at Brooklyn College. She also paints almost daily, sponsors a number of women in 12-step programs, and is actively involved in the lives of her grandchildren. Though she's been successfully engaged in unfolding her calling for over ten years, she still finds her greatest challenge to be showing up everyday, alert, awake, and balanced. As she puts it, "It has taken me a long time to realize, in order to be of service, I have to practice what they tell you during take-off in an airplane: "Put on your own oxygen mask first, then help your neighbor with theirs." It has taken me years to learn to recognize when I was off-center, what caused it, and what I could do about it. Sometimes it's as simple as knowing when I need to take a nap; other times it's as challenging as recognizing that to fix someone else's life ends up in an emotional hangover. In both cases I'm unfit to work with clients or gang members. In other words, I have to be aware of my own issues to be present and available to see yours; only then can I fulfill my intention to be of service to my clients."

Diana has learned to identify the essential elements in her life that she cannot afford to sacrifice without losing her effectiveness, focus or momentum. She's become aware that she needs to get enough sleep, see her grandchildren regularly, hire additional therapists when her work load hits seven clients a day, eat healthy, exercise, listen to music, and go to the theater. She also must allow herself time to enjoy mindless activities like Scrabble or solitaire and share deep emotional and spiritual moments with friends and family. She knows that each of these activities satisfies different emotional requirements and when she fulfills them they act as soul food for her prodigy and her self. When she respects her own needs and acts appropriately, the razor's edge becomes the most pleasurable place to be; when she abandons her needs, it's a slippery slope that leads to unhappiness, anxiety and sadness.

As Diana puts it, "I had to learn to balance what I want to do with what I actually can do, and love myself enough to know when I'm doing too much." To do this, she's had to learn to distinguish old messages like, "Don't start anything you can't finish," that have driven her to physical, emotional or spiritual exhaustion in the past. Now she listens when her body or her feelings tell her, "You're tired, take a break." When she's able to distinguish her unconscious tendencies from her real life, present needs, she remains alert and available to gracefully balance on the razor's edge.

Prodigy Practice #40 – Finding the Razor's Edge.

PART III:

Giving Your Gift, Living Your Calling

CHAPTER 10

THE 12 ARCHETYPES OF SERVICE

The 12 Archetypes of Service represent the unique way in which each of us gives our gift to the world and shares our calling. It's not enough to know what your gift is, or even to be living it halfway. To experience real satisfaction in life, individuals must ultimately develop a channel for giving that resonates with their needs, their passions, and their spirit. Though an individual who is talented in a field may excel, it's not until they've hooked their Gift up with their Primary Archetype of Service that they will be fulfilling their Destiny. For example, if your gift is physics, you can share it through the archetype of The Explorer, like Einstein; or The Problem Solver, like Enrico Fermi; or The Mentor, as do thousands of gifted high school teachers. Until individuals successfully marry their gift with their Archetype (or Archetypes) of Service, they will never fully experience what Abraham Maslow refers to as self-actualization.

As you peruse the list of archetypes below, considering which are your primary archetypes, be aware that the descriptions that follow each of them are a means for you to begin to identify the way you manifest that archetype. You may know you are an activist but find you only relate to "I Voice" and "I Believe" and don't actually feel as though that "I Change" applies to you. On the other hand, though you might relate to only one of the descriptions, you may discover that identifying the one you do not relate to could key you into why you are not manifesting through your archetype. For example, you may realize that you are not engaging in "I Change" because of the fear of the fallout you might have to deal with when you begin "changing" things. For now just acquaint yourself with the list and begin to narrow and identify the Archetypes that you relate to, and the rest will become obvious as you continue reading through this chapter.

THE 12 ARCHETYPES OF SERVICE

THE ALTRUIST – I Give, I Serve, I Love

THE WORKER – I Do, I Work, I Maintain

THE EXPLORER – I Seek, I Discover, I Excel

THE ACTIVIST – I Believe, I Voice, I Change

THE ARTIST – I Reveal, I Design, I Create

THE COLLABORATOR – I Enhance, I Contribute, I Engage

THE NURTURER – I Share, I Care, I Nourish

THE LEADER – I Lead, I Guide, I Direct

THE MENTOR – I Teach, I Support, I Inspire

THE PERFORMER – I Express, I Entertain, I Uplift

THE HEALER – I Heal, I Enhance, I Renew

THE PROBLEM SOLVER – I Organize, I Resolve, I Explain

1. THE ALTRUIST – I Give, I Serve, I Love

The Altruist lives to serve others, often to the exclusion of one's self. Altruists are motivated by powerful feelings of empathy and an unselfish desire to improve the welfare and wellbeing of others. They personally experience the pain, suffering, and lack of their fellow humans (as well as animals and nature itself), as a personal affront, an unacceptable situation. The pure Altruist can be seen in the life of Mother Teresa, who, with no thought of self, dedicated her life to alleviating the pain and suffering of the street people and lepers of Calcutta. She lived for them to make their lives better. Her gift of ministering to those in need and the Altruist archetype were a perfect correspondence.

Altruists include Jimmy Carter and Audrey Hepburn.

2. THE WORKER – I Do, I Work, I Maintain

The Worker is an individual who finds great joy in making others' dreams and visions come into being. Workers love simply *doing*. They are the unsung heroes, the workers who actually create the structure and substance of others' dreams and visions. Depending on the job, they invest their physical labor, emotional support, mental stamina, and general resolve to everything they set out to accomplish. They know their role is pivotal, though often undervalued, and they are actually the ones that make things happen. They live for a job well done, an edifice built, a dream completed, and an operation smoothly run.

Workers include a cafeteria cook, teacher, governor or CEO of a Fortune 500 Company.

3. THE EXPLORER – I Seek, I Discover, I Excel

The Explorer is motivated by the call of what the rest of us refer to as "the unknown." Explorers already sense and know what they are seeking to "discover" and prove to the rest of us. They live to Explore and chart new worlds. Columbus knew he would not sail off the end of the earth. Einstein sensed relativity long before he proved it theoretically. Freud was fully aware of the existence of the unconscious long before others accepted it. Michael Jordan knew he could fly; it just took instant replay for the rest of us to believe.

> *A person is not a thing or a process but an opening through which the Absolute can manifest.*
>
> Marin Heidegger

Explorers are forerunners who live on the leading edge of evolution. They reveal who and what we can become by going there first. They destroy our limiting concepts about who we are, where we're going and what we're capable of. They push the envelope in their discipline. As a group they are inventive, endlessly creative, driven to fulfill their ideals, and whole-heartedly committed to living out their version of reality. They are athletes who exceed expectations with their bodies, pioneers who venture into every dark and unknown corner of our world, or entrepreneurs who invent new products and business models. Explorers discover and reveal the unknown, thus forever transforming our belief systems, ideals and collective agreement about what is real and what is possible. They redefine the laws and ideals by which the rest of us live. They pave the way for the establishment of new agreement realities. They are happiest breaking out in uncharted directions, perfecting their unique way of doing things and exploring our universe.

Even after an Explorer has discovered what they set out to find, they'll usually remain dedicated to seeking and learning everything they can about their discovery and making informed projections of our ultimate potential.

Explorers include Amelia Earhardt, Jonas Salk, Madame Curie, Michael Jordan, Yuri Geller, &, Leonardo da Vinci.

4. THE ACTIVIST – I Believe, I Voice, I Change

The Activist is an individual who believes so strongly in a cause that he or she is willing to fight, and if necessary, to die for it. Activists are not only identified by their passionate and consuming commitment to what they believe in, but also by their willingness to take appropriate actions, even at great personal expense. Whether it's righting an injustice, transforming outworn and demeaning practices, or fighting evil and wrongdoing, Activists will give everything they can to establish justice. They strive for what is equitable and defend what they believe to be the God-given rights of every individual. Gandhi was compelled to eliminate the tyrannical rule and treatment by the British of his countrymen. Susan B. Anthony marched and protested to bring an end to the gross inequality in our electoral process. Rosa Parks took a seat on a bus and changed everything.

5. THE ARTIST – I Reveal, I Design, I Create

The Artist is someone who is compelled to reveal what calls to them from beyond the material world; they do not seek agreement from others as to its validity, reality, or value; they yearn only to capture their inspiration in an aesthetic form for others to experience for themselves. Beethoven was haunted by the music that filled his soul and sought to capture it at all costs. Picasso was compelled to reveal the same fragmented psyche that Freud was busy proving and categorizing. The Artist archetype revels in the act of creating. The pure Artist archetype serves simply and totally by creating.

Artists include Mozart, Georgia O'Keeffe and Marlon Brando.

6. THE COLLABORATOR – I Enhance, I Contribute, I Engage

The Collaborator is an individual who serves by creating, enhancing, and facilitating collective undertakings. Collaborators have a deep need to be a contributing part of a vision, journey or enterprise. They are highly skilled in supporting and enhancing the work of others. Through his uncommon ability to collaborate with scientists, politicians and activists, Al Gore has awakened and alerted the rest of us to the precarious position we inhabit as a species and a planet.

Collaborators excel at making things greater than the sum of their parts. They have enormous respect and admiration for other people's skills; they love the journey involved in collectively achieving a goal; they are driven to enhance the efforts of others and raise the overall quality of the finished product. In the sports world, Magic Johnson was highly respected for the way he collaborated with his teammates, shared the ball and the limelight, and constantly looked to enhance the overall effort of the team. Collaborators are great partners and the ultimate team players.

7. THE NURTURER – **I Share, I Care, I Nourish**

The Nurturer is primarily motivated by the need to care for people, places and things. Nurturers are aware of the fragile nature of human life and do everything they can to make the way smooth for those in need of care. They believe that if they love, care, and support enough, they can overcome any obstacle and solve any problem. Though we associate doctors, nurses, and mothers with The Nurturer archetype, it does not mean they are. A football coach, who is usually associated with the Mentor or Leader archetypes, could excel with a primary archetype of Nurturer and a secondary archetype of Problem Solver. Nurturers are motivated by feelings of sympathy, empathy and agape; their every action is infused with sharing, caring, and supporting. Tony Dungy, the head coach of the Indianapolis Colts football team, is an excellent example of a Nurturer. His reputation for nurturing his players is attested to by the extraordinary number of Pro Bowl players that he has fostered as both a head coach and assistant.

Nurturers might include teachers, hospice workers, nannies and volunteers for charities.

8. THE LEADER – I Lead, I Guide, I Direct

The Leader is an individual who serves others by divining and defining a direction—stepping out in front and motivating others to follow. Napoleon was the preeminent leader. He had a vision, inspired his countrymen to believe it was a noble and important one. Then, from atop his horse, he led the charge and compelled the nation to follow. The Leader archetype almost always shows up in conjunction with another archetype. For example, when you fuse the Leader with the Activist you have a Martin Luther King Jr. Add the Leader to the Worker and you have Cesar Chavez. Marry the Leader to the Explorer and you have Marco Polo.

Leaders include Bill Clinton, Margaret Thatcher, Jack Welch (former CEO of G.E.).

9. THE MENTOR – I Teach, I Support, I Inspire

The Mentor is an individual whose greatest joy comes from helping others to grow, transform, or excel. Mentors are often teachers, coaches, and lecturers. Mentors are highly skilled at any or all, of the following skills: cultivating, developing, training, inspiring and directing. Great Mentors recognize the talent exhibited by their charges and are capable of designing and implementing a precise program to help them fulfill their potential. Consider Phil Jackson and Pat Riley, both average pro-basketball players who did not rise to the top until they activated their Mentor Archetype as coaches. Once they were afforded the opportunity of giving through their primary archetype of Mentor, their real gift was revealed in the numerous World Championship titles their respective teams generated.

> *Follow that will and that way which experience confirms to be your own.*
>
> Carl Jung

Mentors include Ken Blanchard, Julia Cameron (*The Artist's Way*) and many 12-Step Sponsors.

10. THE PERFORMER – I Express, I Entertain, I Uplift

The Performer lives to express, engage, and inspire. Performers are out in front casting a spell, weaving a web, delivering an immersive experience. They are masters at invoking the widest possible range of feelings and emotions in others. They are gifted at sensing an audience's (or individual's) level of involvement and adapting their performance accordingly. What Performers enact and express often inspires the rest of us to examine, expand, and enrich our own lives. Performer Charlie Chaplin engaged us by expressing the full spectrum of emotions, depicting every state of mind and enacting the fragile nature of the human condition. There are also passive Performers, like a muse, whose very presence, the way they carry themselves, move, and act, expresses, engages and inspires those they touch.

Performers include Sarah Bernhardt, Elvis Presley, Houdini and Princess Grace.

11. THE HEALER – I Heal, I Enhance, I Renew

The Healer is an individual who is most comfortable when helping others through their healing process. The joy is palpable. Healers are motivated by a powerful need to assist others to "get better" or "be better." They are often times (though not always) deeply empathetic to others' pain. Healers seek to lessen or alleviate pain and suffering and aim to bring ease to disease. They are most alive when dealing with life or death situations. Healers can be physicians, masseuses, teachers and therapists, but they can also be café owners, salespeople or entrepreneurs. If you're wondering whether you are a Healer, check your Peak Experience list to see if any of the peak experiences were related to saving, bettering, or fixing another's life.

The distinction between healing, nurturing and teaching is motivation. In other words, what is the most all-encompassing motivation behind your desire to help?

Healers include Florence Nightingale, your therapist (massage, psychological, physical etc) and Mary Baker Eddy.

12. THE PROBLEM SOLVER – I Organize, I Resolve, I Explain

The Problem Solver lives to help others to function at the highest, most economical and most efficient level. Problem Solvers can look at a situation and find an elegant, direct, synergistic solution. They can also negotiate the obstacles that have inhibited the desired result. Even when Problem Solvers have no idea how to do or fix something, they know how to find their way to a solution. Problem Solvers are often designers, managers, lieutenants, and craftsmen. Henry Kissinger was one of the most notable Problem Solvers in recent history. As Nixon's "lieutenant" he actually designed and negotiated the solutions to situations that the Leader, Nixon, was unable to accomplish.

Problem Solvers can include engineers, policy makers, city planners and human resources executives.

- Identifying Your Primary and Secondary Archetypes

Though many gifted people spend their entire lives living and giving through a single archetype, most of us have two, three or more archetypes that form the core of our giving. Leonardo da Vinci is one of the most notable examples. Though his primary archetype, the one that motivated and empowered the others, was the Explorer, he was also Artist and Mentor. Over the course of his life, Leonardo da Vinci, expressed himself through each of his primary and secondary archetypes. As he explored all of who he was and his ways of giving, each of his primary and secondary archetypes played a leading role for a time while the others remained active and engaged. By giving full expression to all of his archetypes, da Vinci was not a frustrated Explorer, tortured Artist or failed Mentor, but instead, a fully-integrated and self-actualized human being. His prodigy within achieved full bloom and the gift he gave has continued to inspire the rest of us for five hundred years.

Though your primary archetype(s) do not have to be the primary way you express yourself, it is my experience that unless it plays a significant role in your self-expression you will never fully experience the deepest, most nourishing levels of satisfaction and self-actualization innat to your particular calling. It also happens that over the course of developing and expanding your calling one archetype will offer you more opportunities to share and express your gift than will some of the others. It may be that in the next phase of your calling unfolding, that archetype may move into a secondary or minimal role or be replaced completely by another. Shifting with the times, as dictated by the prodigy within, inspires 1) a deepening of our self-understanding, 2) an extraordinary opportunity to develop all of the aspects of our gift, and 3) a means to process any and all of our unconscious resistance and tendencies, creating ever greater means to be of service in our world.

> *The only ones among you who will be really happy are those who have sought and found how to serve.*
>
> Albert Schweitzer

To discover your primary and secondary archetypes:

- Identify the archetypes you've used or relied upon in the past. These are the ones that felt the most natural in the moment and proved repeatedly to be the most effective and satisfying way for you to share yourself and your gift

- Read the list of archetype "I Statements" (e.g. I Serve, I Nourish, I Design) and observe which statements resonate with your peak experiences, the times you get the greatest satisfaction and enjoyment from giving and sharing.

- Read the archetype descriptions and observe which best suits you.

- Identify personal friends or famous individuals whose ways of giving inspire and resonate with you and identify their archetypes of service.

A friend of mine, Jeff, is happily fulfilling his calling being what he describes as an "enlightened entrepreneur." When he first looked at the list he wondered why the Entrepreneur was not one of the 12 archetypes. When I asked him to review the list to determine which archetypes represented the motivation behind his entrepreneurial endeavors, he determined in each of his businesses his joy came from being the Leader, the Mentor, the Worker and the Altruist. When we discussed his archetypes, Jeff acknowledged as the Leader, each of the descriptors, "I Lead, I Guide and I Direct" applied to him. But as the Mentor, he only resonated with, "I Support and I Inspire" and actually made sure to hire people he wasn't required to employ the "I Teach" aspect of mentoring with. (It's important to note this didn't make Jeff any less the Mentor, only that teaching wasn't how he fulfilled his need within the Mentor archetype.) After Jeff identified his motivation and the way he needs to give, he understood how others could also be entrepreneurs yet have a completely different constellation of archetypes. Another entrepreneur could come together as the Explorer, the Activist and the Worker and another as the Artist, the Problem Solver and the Collaborator. The awareness that entrepreneurs could have a number of different ways to manifest their gift, made Jeff realize he probably would not enjoy his gift nearly as much or, for that matter, be nearly as successful had he not inadvertently discovered his unique archetypes of service.

It's important to understand that no matter what your gift is, you'll have your own unique way of giving. When we actualize our gift and successfully activate and constellate our archetypes, we generate "Soul Food" for our world and ourselves.

Prodigy Practice #41 – My Archetypes: Identify your archetypes.

• To Thine Own Archetypes Be True – Living Your Archetypes

By identifying and giving via your primary Archetypes, you firmly plant yourself on the path of least resistance in regard to discovering and expanding your calling. It's important to understand that even if you're not certain what your gift is, just giving through your archetypes will move you in its direction. As Newton stated, "a body at rest tends to remain at rest, while a body in motion tends to remain in motion." As you give through your archetypes, you naturally gravitate toward giving that which you have most to give. Hence the very act of giving functions as a preliminary means to navigating toward a deeper knowledge and experience of your calling.

> *To the extent that your work takes into account the needs of the world it will be meaningful; to the extent that through it you express your unique talents, it will be joyful.*
>
> *"How To Find Work You Love"*
>
> Laurence Boldt

When people refer to themselves having "never fulfilled their potential," often what they are saying is they have yet to discover and activate their primary archetypes of service. When you know which archetypes most resonate with who you are, you need only begin to share through them to further liberate the prodigy within. By doing so, you not only generate the most nourishing and inspiring way to share your gift with the world, but you also develop a passionate commitment to continue sharing. It is this commitment that, over time, leads to an ever-deepening understanding of your gifts and calling. This in turn generates the incentive to transform any of your unresolved issues that hinder the further unfolding of the prodigy within's plan for you. When you activate your unique avenues for giving, you create the most powerful mechanism for personal transformation and the acceleration of your awakening to who you really are. You come to know how much you have to offer.

For now, don't be concerned if your calling is not being expressed through your primary or secondary archetypes. It is only really a concern when your life doesn't include them. You may find that your calling is expressed through one of your archetypes, while you express another one of your primary archetypes through other hobbies, interests, and passions. Over time, your primary and secondary archetypes will dovetail and enhance your giving. For now, as long as you are even moderately giving yourself through each one of them, their collective impact will enhance every aspect of your life. This in turn will continue to fuel your calling and accelerate the actualization of your Higher Self.

Prodigy Practice #42 – Activate Your Archetypes.

- Being Off-Archetype

We can all relate to the frustration and unhappiness that comes with finding ourselves in a job, or worse yet a career, that requires us to give in a way that is not in alignment with our primary archetypes of service. It generally starts at a very young age when we attempt to please our parents or meet their expectations by trying to be someone we are not. As we grow up, this behavior extends to friends, teachers, jobs and any person or situation where we feel our needs (survival, love, acknowledgment) will not be met if we do not give what we feel is required of us. All the therapy in the world will never uncover the source of your unhappiness if you're off-archetype. For example, your gift is music and your archetypes are Explorer and Collaborator, but you're earning your living as a mix of the Worker/Problem Solver archetypes. To show up for work, when you're not giving through your primary archetypes, you must sublimate your own needs, deny your real feelings and alienate your true Self.

The story of Saul illustrates how one can be attuned to his gift, yet unhappy and unsatisfied with his life. Saul was a child prodigy on the drums. At 12 years old his band opened for the biggest bands in the world. Unfortunately Saul's career was mismanaged and everything fell apart. In fact, he was so discouraged he abandoned sharing his gift until many years later when he was asked to do a drumming circle for parents share day at school. As a result of that one-day, Saul's other primary archetypes, Mentor and Nurturer were revealed to him and his world blew wide open. Soon Saul was doing drumming circles at schools all over town. He now has a foundation that offers drumming workshops for children and adults with emotional problems, learning disabilities, and terminal diseases. By living in alignment with his primary archetypes, Saul now experiences a joy and satisfaction he never experienced when he was only expressing his Performer archetype. The truly telling aspect of Saul's story is that as a result of the opportunities his foundation has af-

> *Each man had only one genuine vocation – to find the way to himself. His task was to discover his own destiny – not an arbitrary one – and live it out wholly and resolutely within himself. Everything else was only a would be existence, an attempt at evasion, a flight back to the ideals of the masses, conformity and fear of ones own inwardness.*
>
> *"Demian"*
> Hermann Hesse

forded him, he's found a way to perform once again. In addition, the foundation has presented Saul with endless opportunities to develop his Collaborator, Explorer, Activist and Healer as well. Today, as Saul tells it, there is no part of his life that has not been touched and transformed by his Being On Archetype. Saul is now the embodiment of his calling, continuously expanding in wonderful and wild new directions.

Another effect of not giving through your primary and secondary archetypes is that the blocked energy most often ends up expressing itself negatively. An Activist who doesn't have a cause to fight for tends to polarize people to the point of starting fights. A frustrated Performer often generates personal dramas (act-ing out) as a means to express the need to act. A Mentor who isn't guiding others often offers others unsolicited advice. Performers need to perform; Activists need a cause to fight for; Mentors need to teach. Being blocked from our primary archetypes not only generates suffering, but also further alienates us from others and from the prodigy within.

Prodigy Practice #43 – Archetype Sabotage: Identify how you deny your archetypes.

- Accelerating Self-Actualization

Once you are giving through your primary archetypes, circumstances will often require you to develop your secondary archetypes. Because you are already experiencing the value you are creating in your world and acquiring the self-esteem that comes with being of service, it will be natural to venture into new archetypes of service that are either uncomfortable or intimidating. When you begin to stretch into undiscovered areas of the Self (your less developed archetypes), you accelerate 1) the integration of the personality, 2) the actualization of the Higher Self, 3) the potency of your giving, and 4) the unpredictable expansion of opportunities to manifest your calling. Through this process of self-actualization, you gain mastery in each of the archetypes and the freedom to give through whichever one will serve the highest end at any given time. Eventually you become facile at giving through whatever archetypes need and situation require.

Scott's story demonstrates how aligning our primary and secondary archetypes accelerate self-actualization. Scott was an out of work actor earning his living as a chef. Obtaining little satisfaction or growth from either endeavor, Scott decided to go back to school to get his teaching credential. As a teacher, his primary archetypes of Mentor and Performer and secondary archetypes, Nurturer and Worker were all activated and integrated. In his first year, he was voted "Best English Teacher" and in his third year he was invited to be the head of the English department. As he continued to enjoy the fruits of his calling, he was offered continuous opportunities to develop his lesser archetypes: Leader, Collaborator, and Problem Solver. Unsure of whether he was the right person to be doing what he was being asked to do, Scott proceeded tentatively. As he processed his feelings and decided to embrace, develop, and apply his lesser archetypes, Scott found himself in situations that led him far beyond teaching. He began to create new programs, new classes,

> *Actually … I am the possessor of unlimited resources. The more I do with them, the more they will grow and cancel out the difficult and painful aspects that now get so much of my attention.*
>
> "One Day At A Time In Alanon"

and new educational prototypes that resulted in the transformation of his school district. In his fourth year the students, faculty, and school board voted him Teacher of the Year. For the first time in his life, Scott felt that he was doing all he was meant to do—that he was actualizing his full potential.

Prodigy Practice #44 – Awaken Your Sleeping Archetypes.

CHAPTER 11

LIVING ON PURPOSE: FULFILLING YOUR DESTINY

Okay, so you're developing your gift and discovering the ways you need to share it with the world. You feel you are beginning to fulfill your potential and you are enjoying the joy and feedback that accompanies it. Life is finally on track in a way you only dared to dream of in the past. So, what's next? Living on Purpose.

As every part of your life begins to come into alignment with your intention to be of service, you begin Living on Purpose. When you are living on purpose you feel:

1. "I am truly guided," whether it be by the prodigy, benevolent intent or a higher power.

2. "Everything I do has value, even when I'm not aware of it,"

3. "Beyond a doubt, I am making a contribution personally, professionally and collectively."

4. Living and giving are an absolute joy and a delicious adventure.

In the Hindu tradition, life is divided into three phases. In the first you are self-centered (just watch any child); in the second you become a "householder," centered on your family and your place in society; and in the third, the final phase, you dedicate the remainder of your life to your spiritual growth and being of service to humanity. In modern western civilizations the first two stages of life follow the same path. From birth and into our 20s, we are focused on satisfying our personal needs, discovering our talents, developing our skills and exploring our passions. In our late 20s, and through our 40s we're consumed with making our mark, achieving our goals, raising a family, striving to excel, accumulating wealth and preparing for what we believe we will require for a comfortable future. The first two phases of life are focused on ourselves, believing, "I am what I do and it is my doing that sustains me."

> *We are called to be architects of the future, not its victims.*
>
> R. Buckminster Fuller

It is in the third stage of life we (in the west) diverge radically from the eastern tradition. In modern society, the final phase of life is represented as the time when you reap the fruit of your labors, sustain yourself on the wealth you have accumulated and enjoy retiring from the continuous pressure of having to produce and earn a living. However, in the last 30-40 years much of the sheen of the "golden years" has faded. Today many people approach their final decades without a nest egg while others discover inflation has rendered their years of saving for "retirement" insufficient. Many arrive at the third phase of life experiencing a spiritual crisis arising from the feeling their life has lacked purpose and meaning and their selfishness has cost them their humanity. Many feel that their selfishness or overactive sense of responsibility has led them away from who they really are and what they were meant to do. The skyrocketing number of men and women suddenly confronted by this "Dark Night of the Soul" is one of the most telling and positive attributes of the times we live in. Telling, because it is indicative of how few people are living their calling, and positive, because it represents us awakening (collectively) to our desire to evolve, be of service, and experience ourselves as contributing members to the well-being of our fellow humans.

Whether you've been successful or not, awakening to this overarching sense of longing—the feeling that something is missing, that "I need to contribute to the greater good"—represents standing at the portal of the final phase of life, giving back. As you begin to embody your calling, discover your way of giving, and experience the joy of living on purpose, you recognize (and acknowledge) yourself as a co-creator and experience living in harmony with your Self, your fellow travelers, and the Spirit of the planet itself. You have successfully begun the transition from survival consciousness to grace. You know, without a doubt, for the first time in your life, "I am here to give, and it is my giving that sustains me."

- Priming the Pump

Giving your gift draws the prodigy out of exile and into the world. Every chance to give your gift feeds the soul, widens your channel and throws opens the floodgates for more opportunities to give. It's called Priming the Pump, and it's as true of the mechanics of water as it is of living on purpose. I know many out-of-work "actors" who do not act. They spend more time complaining about how they can't find (paying?) work than actually acting. For some reason it doesn't occur to them that being in a community play, taking a part in a student film, reading to the elderly or delivering singing telegrams is acting and as such (even though they may not yet be being paid) means they are already living their calling. Any opportunity to share your calling primes the pump and often results in jump-starting your career. Of course, there is a downside to developing places to give your gift away, for no or low pay: you have to give up your alibi of not being able to fulfill your calling.

> *You can get what you want in life if you help enough other people get what they want.*
>
> Zig Ziglar

Over and over I have seen that by learning to say "Yes!" to giving your gift, in any and every possible way, you 1) help the prodigy develop a strong foothold in your life, 2) enhance your ability to attract more opportunities, 3) and increase your sphere of influence. This can occur by volunteering, deferring payment, speaking at your child's school or just plain old-fashioned giving. If you are engaged, in any way, in doing what you love, you will find you are not only rewarded mentally, emotionally and spiritually, but also that you have alerted the universe you are committed to living your giving and embodying your calling. It is not our place nor do we have the global vision to know where our gift is most needed.

Since we can only know who we are, what we have to offer, and that we ache to share our gifts with the world, it is imperative we learn to share our gift whether it pays or not, is perfect or not, measures up to our expectations or not. It is ours to intend, acknowledge, and receive. With each circumstance we embrace, we set the stage, prime the pump, and throw open the floodgates that carry us to ever greater opportunities to give.

Prodigy Practice #45 – Priming the Pump: Kick your passions up a notch.

- The Ongoing Care and Feeding of the Prodigy

A balanced life is one that includes proper nutrition, your ideal forms of exercise, the right relationships, rest, inspiration, play and exploration. You must learn to value and fulfill your basic needs: the ones you require to remain open and available to life as it presents your calling to you in all of its various permutations. In other words, to increase your connection and commitment to the prodigy within, you need only find the things that positively impact your overall well-being and DO THEM, while reducing or eliminating those activities (foods, people, jobs, and addictions) that compromise it.

It's my experience that we've got to have our physical, mental, emotional, and spiritual bodies aligned and tuned up to sustain the prolonged energy, focus and commitment required by the prodigy to fulfill its mission. When we are aligned within ourselves, we are infinitely more effective in our world. For instance, I need a minimum of two yoga classes each week to keep my mind clear, my emotional awareness high, and my body fit. For me, nothing supports my prodigy better than eating smart, exercising regularly, seeking creative outlets, and programming playtime. It's essential for each of us to ask ourselves: What does my prodigy within need? What's the perfect diet, form of exercise, reading materials, creative outlets and relationships? What is it that allows me to remain open and focused on nurturing my prodigy and manifesting my dreams?

In addition to knowing what the prodigy within needs, there's another aspect of prodigy fitness that has to do with learning to process our life experiences in real time. The more contemporary we are, the easier it is to sort our feelings and remain available to the guidance of the prodigy. In other words, take action as close to the time these challenging events or experiences occur. When we allow situations to accumulate, they tend to create interference (background noise) that makes it difficult to get in touch with our true feelings. Even when we are living in "real time" we still tend to file certain things away we will need to deal with later. For example, on the physical level we may have eaten poorly for several weeks (or years) so that the body would require cleansing to eliminate the toxins that have accumulated and undermined our mind/body connection, destroyed our equanimity, and killed our momentum and focus. On the emotional level, we may have been involved in relationships with an employer or loved one where we have had to stuff our feelings. In this kind of a situation, we need to discover effective ways to identify and process these feelings and change the behavior so we stop generating a subterranean stream of negative emotions that continuously pulls us off center. On the mental level, we need to identify expectations, assumptions, projections, antiquated belief systems and obsessive thoughts that live as negative and distracting force in our lives, Whether it's through therapy, 12-step groups, meditation, regular ventures into nature or an inspiring relationship, each of us needs to cultivate the ways and means to live at the speed of life.

> *I'd rather fail at my own life than succeed at someone else's.*
>
> David Whyte

To fully accelerate the embodiment of the prodigy within, you:

1. Can't do it alone. You need to create personal and profes-

sional support for the You that is emerging—support that grounds you in your commitment to the prodigy and reflects back to you a clear vision of your dreams and inclinations.

2. Learn to take really good care of yourself on every level. It's important to understand that this is not a luxury but a necessity and requires daily time to connect with yourself. This self-reflection includes hiking alone, journaling or meditating.

3. Learn to live at the Speed of Life; the speed at which you can balance intake, digestion and elimination. This represents the amount of time and space you require to fully digest your experiences, extract the nutrients (physical, emotional, mental and spiritual), eliminate the wasteful and useless elements and maintain the presence of mind to consciously take the next appropriate action.

Prodigy Practice #46 – 4 Categories of Self-Care:

- Cadres – Building a Sphere of Influence

Building a Sphere of Influence is not networking, but it requires that you recognize, seek out, and form friendships and alliances with individuals (prodigies) who support, champion, and facilitate both their own and your calling. When you meet people who are embodying their prodigy, it's empowering to acknowledge their gift and when appropriate, to offer to share yours. As you reach out to those that are living their giving, you begin to establish interlacing Spheres of Influence. By developing these interlacing Spheres of Influence, you place yourself at the epicenter of readiness, awaiting the time when you are compelled to offer your gift as part of a collective calling.

A group of prodigies gathered together for a period of time, to answer a collective calling and fulfill a singular purpose, is a cadre. A cadre most often is drawn together around the vision of a single person or existing group of prodigies. Cadres are extraordinarily powerful, extremely fluid, vehicles for real change. Prodigies are drawn to existing cadres as needed and then move on when they've completed making their personal contribution. Unlike a government job you get for life, a prodigy's contribution to a cadre lasts only as long as it is required to fulfill the cadre's specific intention. Cadres themselves are extremely fluid groups, coming together for as long as necessary and then (often) dissolving once they have fulfilled their stated purpose.

Tell me with whom you go, and I will tell you what you do.

William Blake

Though cadres are hierarchical, they are truly democratic. Each individual's contribution is perceived and understood as necessary and therefore valued equally. When your contribution is valued, it is easy to give your all, trust the natural unfolding of the intended outcome and experience a deeply spiritual level of nourishment. Cadres are the safest, gentlest and most pleasurable places to embody your prodigy, release the past, and actualize your highest Self. Whether you are the person responsible for initiating a cadre or simply a member, your old patterns, unconscious tendencies and residual karma (unconsciousness surrounding the way past actions motivate current behavior) are naturally revealed without shame or blame and effortlessly transformed within the heightened state of consciousness that permeates a cadre. In addition to transforming karma, it is not unusual to find yourself enjoying prolonged (or recurring) peak experiences, lasting days, weeks or months, while actively involved. In my experience there are few circumstances in life that are as satisfying or as joyful.

When you are a member of a cadre and collaborating with other prodigies, you feel that you are truly blessed, making a significant contribution and living the life God intended you to.

Prodigy Practice #47 – Discover your spheres of influence:

- Branding – Give Your Prodigy, Your Gift and Your Service an Identity

What is it that is unique about you and what you have to offer? Who needs what you have and why do they need it? How do you want to present yourself, your Gift and your service?

When you can answer these questions, you will have begun to define your brand; the unique, specific and enticing way that best represents who you are in the marketplace of life. Your brand is the interface between who you are, those whom you wish to present yourself to (your niche, audience, customer or potential employers) and how you present yourself as the answer to their needs. In the world of advertising, what defines the level of success of two similar products (or services) is how clearly they define and appropriately address the needs of the niche they wish to serve. If you can define the niche that your gift, service and archetypes are geared toward, you will know how to brand yourself. Coke is "the real thing," Pepsi is for a "new generation," and if you use a Macintosh you'll "think different," (like Einstein or John Lennon). Though these are only slogans, they represent and clearly define what they offer and the niche they are going after. When you know your niche, everything you present to the world—photographs, advertisements, lectures, and your personal presentation—are designed to enhance your brand image and the promise you are making.

Now, I realize that many people are challenged to think of branding themselves as they would a product or service. The truth is, even in your personal life, you project an image and therefore an unspoken guarantee of what you stand for and how a relationship with you will enhance and affect others' lives. A trait shared by most individuals living their calling is that who they are and what they say about themselves corresponds perfectly to what they deliver and, often times, with how others perceive them. The concept of branding your calling extends from your business card, your appearance, and your self-assessment to what you do, how you do it and whether you fulfill your brand's promise. As you are perceived as someone capable of delivering on your promise, you will find yourself the recipient of a steady stream of opportunities to manifest your calling. To accomplish this, you don't need to change the way you dress, your haircut or your work, but you do need to consider the niche you present yourself to and the "agreement realities" that define their perceptions of you. It is your responsibility to consider your audience, the impression you make and whether it is in alignment with your intention to manifest your calling. If you are dealing with business people all the time, it might enhance your chances to gain their support, especially when starting out, if you wear a well made suit that fits impeccably. On the other hand, if you have a successful track record, and are seen as a maverick investor, it might enhance your status to wear shorts and a Hawaiian shirt. Either way, how you are perceived is a result born of issues beyond your control and many that are within it. As long as you are

> *We have it in our power to begin the world all over again. A situation similar to the present hath not appeared since the days of Noah until now. The birthday of a new world is at hand.*
>
> Thomas Paine
>
> 1775

true to yourself, your sense of style, creativity and integrity and you are aware of the perceptions of others, you should be able to develop a cohesive, inspiring and inviting brand. By branding yourself in a way that reflects who you really are, casts you in the best possible light, and speaks directly to your ability to fulfill a need (niche), you will be broadcasting your calling.

Prodigy Practice #48 – Define Your Brand: Make your promise.

- Taking It To Market

You are by now aware of your archetypes, developing your gift, discovering places to share it with others and beginning to create your brand. So how do you begin to earn your living—Living on Purpose? The first challenge is to avoid prematurely demanding that the prodigy within be responsible for generating your (entire) income. Think how ridiculous it would be to ask a teenager to support his or her whole family. The best way to jump-start Taking It To Market is to allow where you are earning to pay for where you are going. In other words, keep your day job until your earnings start to shift to your calling. Be aware that it could take a while, but you will begin experiencing various other sources of compensation immediately. Many a client has reported: 1) they began enjoying a new level of joy, acknowledgement and support from all their giving, 2) doors began opening, in the world and at work, to new ways to give, and 3) opportunities to earn related to their gift mysteriously appeared. One other important reason to stay where you are already earning is that unforeseen opportunities will have no trouble finding you. If you are walled up at home, waiting for the phone to ring and scanning the Internet, looking for job opportunities, until your eyeballs bleed, you are not as available to the powerful workings of benevolent intent manifesting through your spheres of influence. I can't tell you how many times friends or clients have found their way to calling related work as a direct result of the people, places, and situations they are exposed to at their current job. Benevolent intent might result from a sale to a business associate, a consulting gig at a company you've been making deliveries to for years, or your boss introducing you to a golf buddy who ends up hiring you, in your spare time, precisely for your calling. Until you are earning a significant portion of your income from your calling, hang where you are with the expectation that benevolent intent will employ your spheres of influence to reveal new ways to earn directly related to your calling. You will know when it's time to quit your existing job (or go part-time), don't force it if you don't want to find yourself squeezed between a rock and your calling.

> *In the new economy, those who pursue their creative passions will have a tremendous edge.*
>
> *"How to Find the Work You Love"*
> Laurence G. Boldt

So how do you begin to take your gift to the marketplace? First and foremost, you prime the pump by exploring every possible way to give your gift for free, cheaply, or in trade. Giving always begets more opportunities to give and turns the tap on for receiving and allowing the marketplace to reveal your niche. The fact is, not every gift translates easily into paid gigs. In fact some may never generate any more than a supplemental income—but that doesn't mean that with a little smarts, a lot of perseverance, and a sincere willingness to give it away, you won't eventually be financially and spiritually supported living your giving. In the worst-case scenario, pursuing avenues for generating income will raise the bar, expand your Spheres of Influence, and shift your consciousness from fear and survival to faith and service.

It would be a mistake to assume for a moment that you have any real idea how you will find your way to the market or how the market will find its way to you. Taking it to market requires you to remain alert to opportunities, think outside of the box, develop a plan and continue just saying yes, even to things that may not appear to be promising financially. Not all income arrives in the form of a job. It may arrive via a fellowship from a foundation, a grant for research, a pilot program, gift or endowment. Additionally, teaching, lecturing, workshops, and consulting are all revenue streams that can grow over time into rivers of opportunity and abundance.

So beyond giving it away and saying "Yes," what else can you do? You can subscribe to journals in your field, talk to head-hunters, go to lectures and workshops given by those who are successful in your arena, Google your precise niche, check the want-ads, hang out with those who are living their giving in a way you admire. You can research areas that might not appear to be related to your gift. For example, as a yoga teacher I could wait forever to get a great time slot to teach (at a specific yoga studio) or I could look into drug rehabilitation centers, prisons, eating disorder clinics, elementary schools, senior facilities and health-conscious corporations. If you are an artist, you could attempt to break into the gallery scene or you could make a deal with your favorite local café to exhibit your work, seek out calendar and greeting card companies, hook up with an ad agency, work on consignment, get your images represented by a stock footage company or make a deal with a foundation that is having a fundraiser and split the proceeds. In any case, the list of ways to earn is endless—its only limits are willingness and creativity.

Prodigy Practice #49 – Revenue Streams: What, where and how can you jump in?

- Grace – Recognizing the Hand of Benevolent Intent

When the prodigy within is the center of your life and you're engaged in sharing your gift with the world, your path becomes infused with an aura of grace. Intentions manifest effortlessly, guidance is revealed mysteriously, opportunities arrive synchronistically, and other prodigies show up consistently. As grace begins to operate in your life, it replaces millions of years of survival-consciousness. As survival-consciousness gives way to grace, you will experience, for perhaps the first time the fulfillment of your needs miraculously being met. When you see the world through the lens of grace, the dramas that accompany survival-consciousness dissolve, no longer usurping your attention, energy or intention.

> *We shall not cease from exploration and the end of our exploring will be to arrive where we started and know the place for the first time.*
>
> *T.S. Eliot*
>
> *Four Quartets*

Now that you are of service to the world, the world supports and serves you. Decisions that used to be difficult become obvious. You rarely feel soiled, abused or manipulated. The people, places, and situations you find yourself attracting (and attracted to) embrace who you are and what you have to offer. You become a beacon of light and a source of inspiration to others, and they love to tell you so. Your presence effects powerful and positive change. You emanate love and you live as a transmitter for the prodigy within's message of hope, purpose and transformation. Like a stone thrown in a quiet pool, the gift you give produces ripples that extend far beyond the scope of your intentions, returning to you as additional support, acknowledgment and opportunity. Living gracefully is living the New World Order. It is literally a higher vibratory level. This higher vibration heals, nourishes, and continues the transmutation of the old self. It's not that you don't feel fear, anger or lack; you do, but they no longer inform your decisions, direction or ability to live your calling.

So, sounds great, but what about today? Today you EXERCISE your ability to recognize

- Your life working professionally, personally and purposefully
- Your intentions materializing
- People supporting you
- Your needs being perfectly met
- How effortlessly you achieve your goals
- The joy that accompanies living gracefully.

The consistent willingness to recognize the new way you inhabit your life will continue to assist your shift into gracefully dancing through the world. With each acknowledgement of grace's place in your life, you erode the old agreement reality that there's "Not enough to go around. I've got to fight for everything I get." As that voice fades it is replaced by the knowing voice of the prodigy, "I am sustained and nourished by my gift and giving."

Prodigy Practice #50: Graceful Living:

- The Realm of the Infinite

The Realm of the Infinite is the place that the prodigy Jesus was referring to when he stated, "These things and more you will do." He was simply reminding his disciples that by following the promptings of the prodigy within, allowing themselves to be guided by benevolent intent and being *grace-full*, they would surpass, in their own unique way, what he had accomplished. By challenging His disciples to fulfill their calling and share their gift with the world, Jesus was suggesting that his disciples would exceed their own and other's expectations. He repeatedly admonished his disciples to live a righteous life (a prodigy-centered life) and promised them if they did that all of the gifts of the "Father" would be given unto them. Ultimately Jesus was challenging each of us to fulfill our own infinite potential, re-unite with our Highest Self and thus become co-creators in the ongoing evolution and spiritualization of our planet.

ACKNOWLEDGEMENTS

When I first began writing *The Prodigy Within* I imagined it would take six months, maybe a year. I had no way of knowing that it would take over four years and require the kind of extraordinary commitment and perseverance I now attribute to prodigies, but had rarely experienced in myself.

From the beginning, I felt called, and from the beginning, the universe guided me to the people who have believed in me, helped me clarify my thoughts and inspired me to keep on keeping on. There's no way I could have made this journey without their love, support and inspiration.

I would like to thank all of my friends and clients who encouraged me through the years of endless head-scratching and re-writing and who were so generous as to allow me to use their personal Prodigy Stories in the book. Leah Komaiko for the wisdom and guidance that grounded me in reality. Trudy Harris, Darwin Carson and Mary Neighbour, extraordinary writers whose insight, care and directness helped me hone my skills and chart my course.

My tireless and loving editors, Katie Stefl, Theresa Stevens, Cindy Bass, Amy Morrisey who respected my feelings, clarified my thoughts, and helped to define my message. And finally, David Walker who made self-publishing a reality by laying out the book, providing a final proofing, and reminding me it was a viable option.

ABOUT THE AUTHOR

Wayne Lehrer has lived The Prodigy Within. At 56, Lehrer has had many successful professions: inventor, educator, health professional, designer, businessman, artist and filmmaker. He has created retail stores and openings for Disney, Viacom, Chrysler, Coca Cola, Northwest Airlines and the Chicago Museum of Science & Industry (voted Best Museum Retail Store in America). He has designed products and launches for various industries including attractions, exhibitions and pavilions for theme parks, casinos and world's fairs. Lehrer has produced and directed openings for HBO, MGM, Fox TV, PBS and CBS Evening News with Dan Rather as well as large events and multimedia presentations worldwide. He wrote, produced, and directed a 3-D animated 70mm film and a children's TV show. He has lectured on holistic health and transformational technologies and helped organize trainings in India. He collaborated in the branding, marketing and naming of dozens of companies. And, though not apparent from this list of his achievements, Lehrer has failed many times on his way to discovering the prodigy within and offering his own unique gift.

Lehrer currently teaches yoga, consults, sculpts marble and leads workshops for individuals and businesses committed to embodying the principles of The Prodigy Within. He is currently developing a line of DVDs (multi-sensory entrainment that enhances brain activity) designed to heal, transform and inspire. In addition to The

Prodigy Within, there will soon be *The Prodigy Within Workbook*, *The Quickening*, *Parenting the Prodigy Within Your Child*, *The Second Half of Life* (a compilation of first-hand prodigy stories gathered from clients and readers), T*he Quest Workshop* and *The Quest* interactive game designed to train future Prodigies.

For further information, workshops and consultations visit: www.prodigywithin.com.

ENDORSEMENTS

Mother Teresa stated that today's society is a culture with a great collective illness. That illness is the poverty of the Soul. Now is the time for the great flowering of humanity and Wayne Lehrer in this book, *The Prodigy Within*, has brought us the tools, heartfelt stories and vision to begin to embody our human greatness.

Bonnie Mansdorf, Founder
Foundation for A Healing Among Nations

The Prodigy Within is brilliant—both spiritually inspirational and a practical toolkit for those yearning to find their life's purpose.

Arthur Jeon, Author
City Dharma

The Prodigy Within is one of those rare books that leads readers to a true understanding of themselves and their essential place in the world. By helping us discover who we are, how we've lived and what our deepest dreams are, Wayne assists us in sourcing from the place of our highest possible destiny.

Alberto Villoldo, PhD., Author
Shaman, Healer, Sage

Just a wonderful book that really made me think about my life and the mindset I need to attain my goals. Through the 12 Archetypes of Service each person is encouraged to consider his/her own life and needs. I realized my calling as worker, artist and explorer.

Karen Perkins
High School Teacher

Harnessing his vast experience and the power of mythology, Wayne Robert Lehrer has written a clear, encouraging and deeply satisfying how-to book that offers readers at every stage of their journey opportunities to deepen their connection with their authentic selves.

Cedering Fox
Founder of WordTheatre

Wayne's remarkable book functions like a personal GPS system for those seeking change: He helps to pinpoint your present location and provides step-by-step guidance towards your intended location.

William D Bauer, PhD
Supervising Analyst at Newport Psychoanalytic Institute

How may I be of service? In asking this question and striving to discover the best in himself, Lehrer has fully claimed his own authenticity and created a down-to-earth and wisdom-filled guide for each of us in our journey to find the gifts of our truest self. With the benevolent intent, open heart and pure spirit of Parsifal, Lehrer offers himself to the world around him in this brilliant treatise of self-actualization.

Jennifer Lehr, MFT

Rarely does an author take you to the edge of yourself. A gift disguised in a challenging journey. *The Prodigy Within* offers the tools you need to increase self-awareness, personal achievement and uncover your "Calling." Don't miss this opportunity to read such a gem. It will leave you ready to begin the journey.

Fireball Tim Lawrence
Movie Car Designer/Entreprenuer

"Wayne is one of my real-life heroes as a self-actualizing person and a writer/artist. As a consultant to my company he brings enthusiasm and out-of-the-box solutions coupled with incisive analysis and insight. Wayne finds the balance between nurturing our creative and spiritual aspirations and challenging us to business success."

David Mumm
Director of PowerLearn Technologies

The Prodigy Within is a life-changing book. During a time when I was at a major crossroads in my life, Lehrer's principles have not only led me to discover the prodigy within myself, but have helped me to make better decisions that have brought me closer to my calling. Since my reading of this book, I have seen wondrous results pertaining to my writing career. It was not the path I thought I would follow, but instead, the path I was meant to follow. Since then, I have been achieving more success than ever.

Theresa M. Heim

Freelance writer/Author

BIBLIOGRAPHY

The Art and Life of Georgia O'Keeffe Jan Garden Castro ©1985
Crown Publishers Inc. New York

Edison: A Biography Matthew Josephson ©2003
History Park Club

Picasso Carsten-Peter Warncke ©2001
Tashen-Koln, Germany

Searching for Bobby Fisher ©1993
Paramount Pictures

Van Cliburn: A Biography Howard Reich and Van Cliburn ©1993
Thomas Nelson, Nashville

Bill Graham: A Parable of American Righteousness Gerald Clarke © 1979
Little Brown, Boston

Capote: A Biography Gerald Clarke © 1988
Simon & Schuster, NY

What Makes the Great Great Denis P Kimbro Ph.D. Doubleday NY
©1998

The Soul's Code James Hillman ©1984
Random House Inc, NY

Heading Toward Omega: In Search of the Meaning of the Near-Death Experience Kenneth Ring ©1984 NY

The Buddha David Kherdian ©2004
Cloud Press

I and Thou Martin Buber (Translation Smith pg 59) ©1958
(Simon & Schuster, NY) Copyright date and holder: Scribner 1958

PRODIGY WITHIN PUBLISHING

For information or to order additional books or other Prodigy products and services please visit our website at **www.prodigywithin.com**

PRODIGY WITHIN PUBLISHING

1112 Montana Ave. #506
Santa Monica, CA. 90403
www.prodigywithin.com

PRODUCTS AND SERVICES

BOOKS

- ❍ The Prodigy Within: The Quest to Discover Your Life's Purpose
- ❍ The Prodigy Within Workbook: Uncovering Your Life's Purpose

CDS

- ❍ Prodigy Yoga—Beginner and Intermediate Yoga CD's
- ❍ Prodigy Meditation Series—5 CD's, 12 minutes each, designed to enhance your prodigy, focus your attention, activate your intuition and clear negative thought patterns.

COACHING AND WORKSHOPS

- ❍ Prodigy Coaching—Personal & Professional Life Coaching, Business Coaching and Consultations.
- ❍ Prodigy Workshops and Seminars—Activating your life's purpose, enhancing personal well-being and accelerating self-actualization.

ART

- ❍ Prodigy Sculpture—Original marble and bronze sculpture.
- ❍ Prodigy Art—Original art limited edition "Light Paintings" in giclee format.

Made in United States
Orlando, FL
13 November 2025

72444810R00142